3

Christ Our Life

We Believe

AUTHORS
Sisters of Notre Dame of Chardon, Ohio

Sister Mary Theresa Betz, S.N.D.
Sister Mary St. Leo DeChant, S.N.D.
Sister Mary Kathleen Glavich, S.N.D.
Sister Mary Patricia Lab, S.N.D.
Sister Mary Andrew Miller, S.N.D.
Sister Jeanne Mary Nieminen, S.N.D.

THEOLOGICAL ADVISOR
Sister Agnes Cunningham, S.S.C.M.

CONSULTANTS
Reverend Edward H. Konerman, S.J.
Reverend Monsignor Joseph T. Moriarty

GENERAL EDITOR
Sister Mary Kathleen Glavich, S.N.D.

LoyolaPress.
CHICAGO

Nihil Obstat:	The Reverend John F. Loya, M.Div., M.A., Censor Deputatus
Imprimatur:	The Most Reverend Anthony M. Pilla, D.D., M.A., Bishop of Cleveland

Given at Cleveland, Ohio, on 5 March 1996

The *Nihil Obstat* and *Imprimatur* are official declarations that a book or pamphlet is free of doctrinal or moral error. No implication is contained therein that those who have granted the *Nihil Obstat* and *Imprimatur* agree with the contents, opinions, or statements expressed.

Christ Our Life found to be in conformity

The Ad Hoc Committee to Oversee the Use of the Catechism, National Conference of Catholic Bishops, has found this catechetical series, copyright 1997 and 2002, to be in conformity with the *Catechism of the Catholic Church*.

© 1997, 2002 Loyola Press and Sisters of Notre Dame of Chardon, Ohio
Printed in the United States of America.
ISBN: 0-8294-1548-3

Dedicated to St. Julie Billiart, foundress of the Sisters of Notre Dame, in gratitude for her inspiration and example

Acknowledgments

This present revision of the Christ Our Life series is the work of countless people. In particular, we acknowledge and thank the following for their roles in the project:

- The Sisters of Notre Dame who supported the production of the Christ Our Life series, especially Sister Mary Joell Overman, S.N.D.; Sister Mary Frances Murray, S.N.D.; and Sister Mary Margaret Hess, S.N.D.
- The Sisters of Notre Dame and others who over the past twenty years have shaped, written, and edited editions of the Christ Our Life series, in particular Sister Mary de Angelis Bothwell, S.N.D., the former editor
- Those who worked on different stages involved in producing this edition, especially Sister Mary Julie Boehnlein, S.N.D.; Sister Linda Marie Gecewicz, S.N.D.; Sister Mary Beth Gray, S.N.D.; Sister Joanmarie Harks, S.N.D.; Sister Rita Mary Harwood, S.N.D.; Sister Mary Nanette Herman, S.N.D.; Sister Mary Andrew Miller, S.N.D.; Sister Mary Catherine Rennecker, S.N.D.; and Sister Mary St. Jude Weisensell, S.N.D.
- Those catechists, directors of religious education, priests, parents, students, and others who responded to surveys, returned evaluation forms, wrote letters, or participated in interviews to help improve the series

Scripture selections are taken from *The New American Bible,* copyright © 1991, 1986, 1970 by the Confraternity of Christian Doctrine, Washington, D.C., and are used by license of copyright owner. All rights reserved.

Excerpts from the English translation of *Rite of Baptism for Children* © 1969, International Committee on English in the Liturgy, Inc. (ICEL); excerpts from the English translation of *A Book of Prayers* © 1982, ICEL; excerpts from the English translation of *Book of Blessings* © 1988, ICEL. All rights reserved.

English translation of *Gloria in Excelsis*, The Nicene Creed, The Apostles' Creed, *Gloria Patri, Benedictus, Magnificat* by the International Consultation on English Texts.

"We Gather Together" [first verse] by Omer Westendorf. Text copyright 1970, World Library Publications, a division of J. S. Paluch Company, 3825 N. Willow Road, Schiller Park, IL 60176. All rights reserved. Used with permission.

All attempts possible have been made to contact the publisher for cited works in this book.

Photographs

© **Artville LLC.** (p. 171); © **Sr. Mary Theresa Betz, S.N.D.** (p. 174A); © **José Carillo/PhotoEdit** (p. 130); © **Cleo Freelance Photography** (pp. 3 bottom, 36 right, 39 top, 76 top and middle left, 82 top, 106, 145 bottom left); © **Comboni Missionaries** (p. 85); © **Corbis Corp.** (pp. 20, 99); © **Corel Corporation** (p. 11); © **Jim Cummins/FPG International LLC.** (p. 9); © **DeJuanes/PHOTRI** (p. 51); © **Demetz Art Studio** (p. 28A); © **Gail Denham** (pp. 61 bottom left, 97); © **Mary Kate Denny/PhotoEdit** (p. 2); © **Diamar Interactive** (p. 167 bottom left); © **Digital Stock Corp.** (pp. 33, 34 middle, 37 top, 66 middle center and middle right and bottom, 80 bottom, 82 bottom, 131, 147); © **Laura Dwight/PhotoEdit** (p. 69); © **EyeWire** (p. 4); © **Myrleen Ferguson/PhotoEdit** (pp. 34 bottom, 39 bottom, 76 bottom, 81 left, 89 left, 150, 164 top); © **Jeff Greenberg/PhotoEdit** (p. 116); © **Sister Rita Mary Harwood, S.N.D.** (p. 52 bottom); © **K-6/ProFiles West** (p. 199); © **George A. Lane** (p. 66 top and middle left); © **Michael Newman/PhotoEdit** (pp. 29, 112); © **Our Lady of the Rockies Foundation** (p. 166); © **Photo Disc, Inc.** (pp. 19 top right, 37 bottom, 61 top right and middle right and bottom right, 62A, 63, 76 middle right, 80 top, 83, 89 right, 98, 100, 102, 107, 122, 128 top, 145 top and bottom right, 174, 183); © **Eugene D. Plaisted, O.S.C./Crosiers** (pp. i, 34 top, 47, 133); © **Mark Richards/PhotoEdit** (p. 167 bottom right); © **Scala/Art Resource, N.Y.,** Titian's *The Assumption of the Virgin*, Venice, Santa Maria dei Frari (p. 165); © **James L. Shaffer** (pp. 13, 61 top left, 82 bottom, 139); © **Skjold Photographs** (pp. 57, 157); © **Stacia Timonere** (p. 167 top left); © **Wide World Photos, Inc.** (p. 144); © **W. P. Wittman Limited** (pp. 1, 3 top, 6, 19 middle left and bottom, 32, 36 left, 39 middle, 41, 48, 52 top, 60, 64, 74, 81 right, 95, 128 bottom, 142, 153, 155, 159, 162, 167 top right).

Artwork *(body)*

Diana Bush (pp. 50, 69, 79, 89, 107, 109, 141, 151, 172, 173 right); **Jim Cummins** (pp. 30, 42, 43, 45, 46, 98, 103); **Don Dyen** (pp. 5, 7, 11 bottom right, 12 top right and bottom, 16–17, 24, 67, 68, 71, 72, 73, 75, 78, 84–85, 87, 163); **Len Ebert/PC&F Inc.** (pp. 15, 56, 94A, 96, 110 bottom, 116); **George Hamblin/Steven Edsey & Sons** (p. 174C); **Diane Johnson** (pp. 8, 20, 32, 35 top right and bottom, 49, 65, 104, 120, 140, 148, 170); **Arist Kirsch** (p. 10); **Laser Type & Graphics** (pp. 26 bottom, 27 top left, 33, 77, 90, 91 left, 92, 97, 108, 113 bottom, 118, 132, 164, 168); **Betty Maxey** (pp. 18, 21, 53, 59, 105, 117, 156); **Eileen Mueller Neill & Kelly Neill** (pp. 62C, 174D); **Kevin Peschke** (pp. 132A–132D); **Proof Positive/Farrowlyne Assoc., Inc.** (pp. 11 top left and top right, 12 top left and middle left, 19, 66, 91 right, 154); **Sally Schaedler** (pp. 14, 22–23, 27 top right, 31, 35 top left, 40, 54–55, 88, 106, 111, 113 top, 114, 115, 119, 121, 123, 124, 126–127, 129, 134, 135, 136, 137, 138–139, 143, 149, 152); **Ralph Smith** (pp. 146, 175, 176); **Carol Tornatore** (pp. 26 top, 38); **Robert Voigts** (pp. 36, 62, 107, 110 top, 173 left).

Artwork *(perforated section)*

Diana Bush (pp. 3, 8, 10, Scripture Booklet); **Bill Gorman** (pp. 6, 7, Scripture Booklet); **Diane Johnson** (p. 1, Reconciliation Booklet; p. 3, Lent Booklet); **Arist Kirsch** (Jesse Tree); **Robert Korta** (Rosary Booklet illustrations; p. 2, Scripture Booklet); **Laser Type & Graphics** (p. 12, Scripture Booklet); **Robert Voigts** (pp. 1, 2, 6, Reconciliation Booklet; p. 1, Advent Booklet; p. 1 ivy, Lent Booklet); **Bill Wise** (p. 1, Lent Booklet; p. 11, Scripture Booklet); all punchouts by **Bill Wise** except the portrait of Jesus, by **Bill Gorman.**

Cover design by Donald Kye.
Cover art © Eugene D. Plaisted, O.S.C./Crosiers.

04 05 06 07 Web 7 6 5 4

LOYOLAPRESS.

3441 N. Ashland Avenue
Chicago, Illinois 60657
(800) 621-1008

CONTENTS

3

Notes to Parents — iv

Unit 1 God Calls Us to Faith — 1
1. God Calls Us — 2
2. God Calls Us to Use Our Gifts — 9
3. We Are God's Holy People — 14
4. Mary Is Called to Be God's Mother and Ours — 18
5. We Are Called to Follow Jesus — 22

Family Feature — 28A

Unit 2 Jesus Is with Us on Our Way — 29
6. God Shares the Wondrous Life of Grace — 30
7. The Holy Spirit Lives within Us — 35
8. God Blesses Contrite Hearts — 40
9. God Forgives Us in the Sacrament of Reconciliation — 45
10. God's Family Celebrates the Eucharist — 51
11. The Eucharist Is a Gift — 57

Family Feature — 62A

Unit 3 God Is Great and Good — 63
12. We Believe God Keeps Promises — 64
13. God Is Powerful and Loving — 71
14. God Is Holy and Great — 78
15. God Is Just and Merciful — 87

Family Feature — 94A

Unit 4 God's Plan Is a Plan of Love — 95
16. God Created People to Share His Life — 96
17. God Sent His Son Jesus to Live among Us — 102
18. Jesus Revealed the Kingdom of God — 111
19. Jesus Came to Give Life — 119
20. God's Kingdom Is a Kingdom of Love — 126

Family Feature — 132A

Unit 5 Jesus Brings Us to the Kingdom of God — 133
21. Jesus Suffered and Died for Us — 134
22. Jesus Is Risen — 142
23. Jesus Christ Is Lord and King — 149
24. Jesus Gives His Spirit to the Church — 156
25. We Belong to the Kingdom — 162

Family Feature — 174A

Maps: The Lands of the Old Testament — 175
Palestine in the Time of Jesus — 176

Glossary — 177

Index — 181

Supplement — 183
- Reconciliation Booklet
- An Advent Project for the Family
- Sharing Lent as a Family
- The Jesse Tree
- Rosary Booklet
- Scripture Prayer Booklet

Cutouts

Notes to Parents

Goals of This Year's Program
This year your child will be learning how God calls us to faith and eternal life with him as members of the faith community, the Church. The focus of this year's study is faith—belief and trust in our all-knowing and all-loving God. The children are presented with the mysteries of faith that we profess in the Creed. Through Old and New Testament events they learn of God's saving love for his people and the truths of our faith. It is hoped that your child will respond with a trusting, joyful surrender to God and an acceptance of all that God has taught us.

Format Designed for a Family Program
Because your faith makes a profound impact on your child, the Christ Our Life series provides a Family Corner feature at the end of each chapter. Usually a chapter is presented in class each week. The activities in the Family Corner encourage you to nurture your child's faith by sharing your own response to God. The Family Corner begins by stating the goals of the chapter. Family activities that promote these aims are listed under four topics:

Read suggests a Scripture reference related to the topic of the chapter.

Discuss provides questions to help you apply the Scripture reading to daily life.

Pray sums up the message for the week in a short prayer that everyone can pray daily. This prayer can be printed and posted on the refrigerator or a mirror. You may add it to meal prayers or other family prayers.

Do provides ideas for sharing at meals and for other family activities related to the message of the chapter. You may wish to read all the suggestions to the family and then decide which one or ones to do that week. You may also wish to choose other activities that family members suggest.

You are urged to help your child evaluate his or her growth at the end of each unit by discussing with him or her the goals on this page. Each of the units in this book ends with four Family Feature pages that suggest family customs and provide review activities.

You can also help your child master the We Remember section at the end of each chapter.

Unit 1: God Calls Us to Faith, pages 1–28
❑ I am using my talents to bring joy to others.
❑ I can say the Scripture verses on pages 2 and 3.
❑ I know the five helps to holiness on page 15.
❑ I can pray the rosary.

Parent's signature _____

Unit 2: Jesus Is with Us on Our Way, pages 29–62
❑ I know the five ways to live the life of grace given on page 33.
❑ I know the Act of Contrition by heart.
❑ I examine my conscience every night.
❑ I celebrate the Sacrament of Reconciliation at least every few months.
❑ I am reverent as I receive Holy Communion.

Parent's signature _____

Unit 3: God Is Great and Good, pages 63–94
❑ I know the Apostles' Creed.
❑ I pray every morning and evening.
❑ I honor God's name and all holy things.
❑ I celebrate Sunday by taking part in the Eucharist and by trying to bring joy to others.
❑ I show respect, care, and concern for all—especially babies, the sick, and the elderly.
❑ I respect the gifts of the earth by caring for them and by sharing them with others.

Parent's signature _____

Unit 4: God's Plan Is a Plan of Love, pages 95–132
❑ I can tell the story of Jesus' birth.
❑ I turn to Jesus for help.
❑ I love, respect, and obey my parents and others who care for me.
❑ I forgive and pray for those who hurt me.
❑ I do what is right, even if I must suffer for it.

Parent's signature _____

Unit 5: Jesus Brings Us to the Kingdom of God, pages 133–174
❑ I can tell how Jesus suffered and died.
❑ I pray and sacrifice for others and help those in need.
❑ I do things that make for peace at home, and I pray for peace throughout the world.
❑ I pray to Mary and the saints and for the holy souls in purgatory.

Parent's signature _____

God Calls Us to Faith

UNIT 1

God calls each person to have faith and take part in his plan of salvation. The children are led to explore God's unique love for them and to discover the talents God has given them to fulfill his plan. Under the guidance of the Holy Spirit, they learn from Mary's example to respond willingly to God's call. They are challenged to follow Jesus as his disciples, spreading the Good News and promoting God's kingdom of peace and justice on earth, as they journey toward their destiny—eternal happiness in heaven.

God Calls Us

God Calls Us by Name

"Hi, Marty!" "Tina!" "Mario!" Excited voices rang out as friends greeted each other after vacation.

Leah felt strange and alone. No one called her name. No one knew her. Then she heard "Leah!" and looked up. Miss Link called out, "Boys and girls, this is Leah Suh. She's in our class this year. Leah has come from Miami, Florida."

"Hi, Leah!" "Welcome, Leah!" children called from all parts of the room. Leah smiled as she looked around. Everyone called her by name. Now she "belonged."

- When have you felt strange and alone? How do you feel when someone calls you by name?
- What makes you feel you "belong"?

God calls us by name. God knows us because he made us. We belong to God.

God says,
"I have called you by name: you are mine."

Isaiah 43:1

2

The Ruiz Family

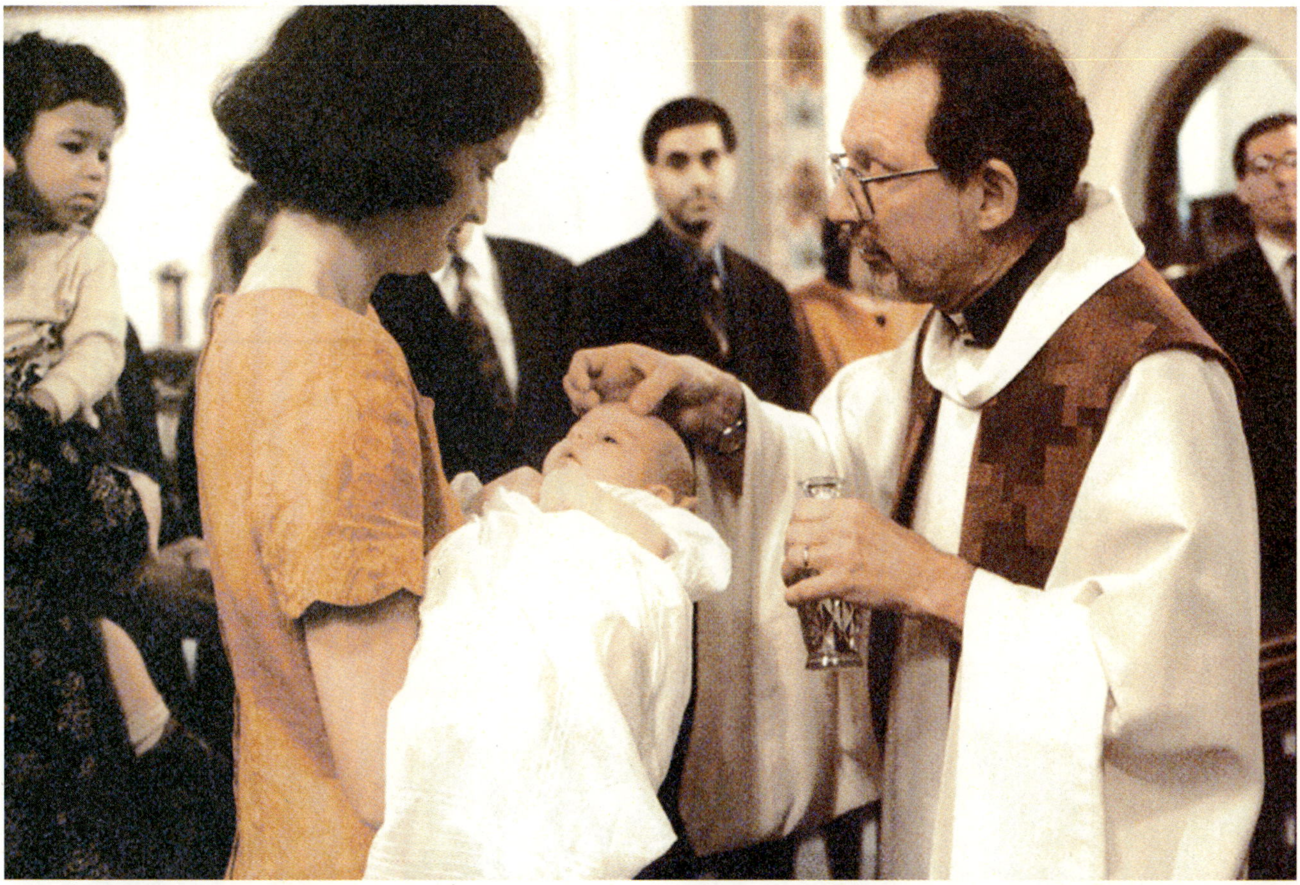

You belong to your family at home. When you were baptized, you joined another family, the Church. Now you are called a Christian and a Catholic. You belong to the big Christian family of people who **believe** in Jesus.

You also belong to the great human family of people all over the world. All of these families belong to God.

Write the letter that comes after the given one. Find out what God says to us.

"I will be your ___ ___ ___ , and you
             F   N   C

will be my ___ ___ ___ ___ ___ ___ ___ ."
           O   D   N   O   K   D
                              Leviticus 26:12

My Family

God Called Abram to Believe

Did you ever have to leave your home and move to a new one? How did you feel?

A long time ago God called a man named Abram. God said, "Leave your home and your country. Go to the land I will show you. I will make of you a great nation."

Abram believed that God would take care of him. He did as God told him. He went to the new land.

Then God spoke to Abram again. He gave him the land and said, "Look up at the sky. Count the stars if you can. The children of your family will be as countless. You shall be called Abraham, and your wife shall be called Sarah. You and Sarah will have a son."

Abraham believed what God said. Although he and Sarah were very old, they had a son. They called him Isaac. He was a great joy to them.

Abraham always believed in God's loving care. He did what God asked even when it was hard. God also calls us to believe in him, even though we cannot see God.

At Baptism we received the gift of **faith.** It helps us to believe in God. We believe that God made us and that we belong to him. We believe that God takes care of us in everything that happens. We believe that we can live with God forever.

Just as God spoke to Abraham, he speaks to us in our hearts. We can come to know God better. Then we will try to do what God tells us even when it is hard. With faith we trust God to do what is good for us. We know God wants us to be happy.

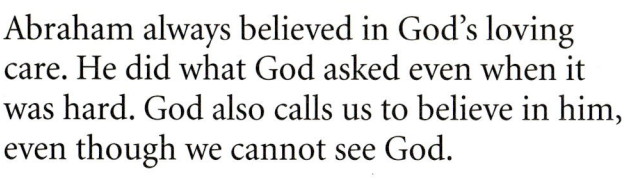

God Calls You to Believe

Abraham did what God asked because he had faith. He knew and loved God. You received the gift of faith at Baptism when you became a Christian. Do you do what God wants?

Imagine that the following things happen to you. Write what God calls you to say and do.

1. Your mother calls you when you are watching a favorite television program. She wants you to clean your room.

What will you say?

_____

_____

What will you do?

_____

_____

2. Your teacher tells you to work a page in your math book for homework. Math is hard for you, and you don't want to do it. Your friend, who is good at math, offers to let you copy his answers.

What will you say?

_____

_____

What will you do?

_____

_____

Draw a picture of yourself doing something God asks you to do.

6

God Called Ruth to Believe

Ruth lived in a country where people believed in false gods. Her husband and his mother, Naomi, told Ruth about God. When Ruth's husband died, she lived with Naomi. She was kind to Naomi and helped her in many ways.

One day Naomi decided to go back to the place where she had been born, Bethlehem. Ruth loved her and wanted to go with her. She said,

> "Wherever you go, I will go.
> Where you live, I will live.
> Your people shall be my people,
> and your God my God."
> adapted from Ruth 1:16

Ruth went with Naomi. In the new country she worked hard every day. She gathered grain in the fields of a man named Boaz.

Boaz was good and kind. Before long he married Ruth, and they were very happy together. God blessed them with a son. Ruth became the great-grandmother of King David. Into the family of David, many years later, Jesus the Savior was born.

God Called Ruth to Believe

7

You joined the family of Jesus, the Church, when you were baptized. Since then you have been called by two special names to show that you belong to the Church. What are they?

Print these names in the puzzle.

We Remember

What does God call us to do?
God calls us to believe in him and to do what he asks.

Words to Know
faith   believe

We Respond

I know that God is with me.
In God I trust.
    adapted from Psalm 56:10, 12

FAMILY CORNER

God calls us to take part in his plan of salvation; God promises his help and blessing if we trustingly respond to his call. Abraham and Ruth are models of fidelity to God's call. They show us that having faith means obediently doing whatever God asks, confident that he always brings us to a fuller, richer life when we faithfully follow his ways.

 Read
Isaiah 43:1–3

Discuss
- What does this reading tell us about God's love?
- Does God promise always to protect us from difficulties?
- What good things can you name that God has given your family?

 Pray
I have called you by name: you are mine. Isaiah 43:1

Do
- Find out the meaning of each family member's name.
- Make a photo collage of your family. Print the words of Isaiah 43:1 around it.
- Ask your child to share the stories of Abraham and Ruth. Discuss what was most difficult for Abraham and Ruth when they each heard God's call.
- Relate the difficulties experienced by Ruth and Abraham to those your family has experienced.

❏ Signature

2 God Calls Us to Use Our Gifts

God Gives Us Special Gifts

Mr. Benson was returning the science booklets the children had made. He called Jenny. "You did excellent work, Jenny. You even wrote about six animals rather than four. You deserve this A."

As Joe came to his desk, Mr. Benson smiled. He praised Joe for the border of little animals Joe had drawn on the cover. "You should be proud of the B+ you got on your book," Mr. Benson said.

But when Mr. Benson called Lottie, he did not look pleased. Lottie had just copied the paragraph about each animal from her science book. Her cover was blank. "I'm sorry, Lottie," Mr. Benson said, "I cannot give you a grade. You will have to make a new booklet."

Who had talent in art? _____

Who had a gift for writing? _____

Who had a gift for teaching? _____

Why don't we know what Lottie was good at? _____

_____

_____

9

God gave all of us talents or gifts that make us special.

Circle the words below that name your special abilities. Write something else special about you in the "What else?" block. Then finish the sentences.

I like _____ .

I am good at _____ .

Something special about me is _____ .

How can you use your talents to praise God and help others?

David Used His Talents

David was a famous king in Abraham's family. He used his gifts to praise God and help God's people. We could give him the following awards.

David was good at using a slingshot. Once he had to fight a giant named Goliath. When David struck the giant on the forehead with a stone, Goliath fell to the ground dead. David used his skill to save his country. He gave glory to God.

David took good care of his father's sheep in Bethlehem. He killed a lion and a bear that attacked them. Samuel once came looking for a new king. Young David was called in from the fields. Samuel knew that David's heart pleased God. He poured oil on David's head. This was a sign that God had chosen David.

David wrote psalms of praise and thanks. He played his music on the harp to cheer up King Saul. Once he even danced in the street to honor God. We still sing David's songs today.

David was crowned king after King Saul. He won the love of all the people. He asked God to stay with him and rule with him. He served his country well as its leader.

Print the missing words in the puzzle. The sentences and the Word Bank will help you.

1. A king anointed as a boy was _____ .
2. A special ability is called a _____ .
3. God made us special because God _____ us.
4. Talents are special _____ from God.
5. We use our talents for _____ and others.

```
        D _ _ _ _
        _ a _ _ _ _
        _ _ v _ _
        _ i _ _ _
        _ _ d
```

Word Bank
God   loves   talent   gifts   David

Putting Talents to Use

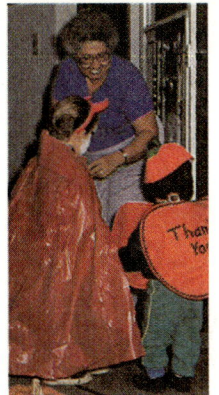

These children are not asking for Halloween treats this year. They are collecting money for poor children in other countries.

How are they using their talents to honor God and to help and give joy to others?

We Remember

Why has God given you talents?
God has given me talents to praise him and help others.

We Respond

I shall praise the LORD all my life.
Psalm 146:2

FAMILY CORNER

Each person fulfills God's plan differently. To aid us in doing his will, God gives us the necessary gifts and talents. He expects us to develop them as best we can and use them for his praise and glory, our own good, and the good of others.

 Read
Matthew 25:14–30

Discuss
- What are the special talents God has given to each member of your family?
- How can these talents be used in the home?
- How can members use their talents to help the Church, school, and place you live?

 Pray
All for you, Most Sacred Heart of Jesus!

Do
- Present a family talent show.
- Make gifts or tray favors for shut-ins and hospital patients.
- Make homemade Christmas gifts.
- Read the story of Johnny Appleseed and discuss how he used his talents for the good of others.

❏ Signature

13

3 We Are God's Holy People

God Calls Us to Be Holy
When God our Father made us, he called us to be **holy.** God called us to **know, love,** and **serve** him. God called us to care for his creation and for all people. This is the way to happiness.

Long ago Jesus showed us how to know, love, and serve the Father. Today Jesus is still with us in his Spirit and in his Church. He helps us answer God's call to become his holy people. We help one another to be holy and happy.

A Heart like God's
Fill the heart with words that finish the sentence.

To be holy means to _____ .

St. Francis Answered God's Call

Francis was a rich young man. He loved to have good times. Then one day he saw what was really important in life. After that Francis gave away his belongings. He cared for the sick and the poor. He loved God and praised him for all the things in creation. Francis became a holy man and a much-loved saint.

Brother Francis (A Play)

Cast   Storyteller   Brother Juniper   Brother Bernard
           Brother Francis   Brother Leo   Birds (any number)

Storyteller: One day long ago, St. Francis and some of his friends were walking along a road.

Brother Bernard: Brother Francis, look at the field over there! It is filled with all kinds of birds.

Storyteller: St. Francis walked to the field. The birds did not fly away. Instead, they gathered around him. St. Francis knelt down and began to preach to them.

Brother Francis: My little ones, God made you and cares for you. You need not plant because he feeds you. God lets you build your nests in his trees. He gave you wings so that you can fly high in his sky. Your feathers keep you warm in winter. With your beautiful voices you can praise God for his goodness!

Storyteller: St. Francis stood up and blessed the birds with the Sign of the Cross. All the birds flew away, praising God with their songs.

Brother Juniper: Brother Francis, the birds seem to understand what you tell them.

Brother Francis: Yes, and they praise God for his goodness. God is good to us too. He loves and cares for us even more than for the birds. God has called us to be holy. He sent his Son Jesus to show us how to know, love, and serve him. We can be happy forever with God in heaven.

16

Brother Leo: Let's praise God now for his goodness to us.

All the Brothers: Be praised, O God, for all your goodness!

Brother Juniper: Bless us too, Brother Francis.

Storyteller: St. Francis made the Sign of the Cross over his brothers. They walked on with joyful hearts.

Word to Know
holy

We Remember

What is the way to eternal happiness?
The way to eternal happiness is to know, love, and serve God.

Who shows us how to be holy?
Jesus shows us how to be holy. He helps us through his Spirit and his Church.

We Respond

God chose us in Christ to be holy and spotless in his sight.
adapted from Ephesians 1:4

FAMILY CORNER

God calls us to be his holy people and gives us his Son, our Way, Truth, and Life. Jesus became man to show us how to live a holy life and teach us the way to the Father. Through his Church, guided by the Holy Spirit, he leads, strengthens, and forms us into God's holy people.

 Read
John 14:6–9

Discuss
- How can we know what God is like?
- How can the saints help us become holy? Name some saints.
- How can we help one another know God better? love God more? serve God well?
- Do you know anyone who is holy? Why do you think that person is holy?

 Pray
Holy Family, make our family holy.

Do
- Take turns telling something you know about Jesus. Read the Bible as a family—a few minutes a day or at some special time each week.
- Discuss whether your use of television helps you become more like Jesus.
- Bring happiness to a sick or an elderly friend by a cheerful visit.
- Ask your child to share the story of St. Francis. Dramatize the play on pages 16 and 17.

❑ Signature

4 Mary Is Called to Be God's Mother and Ours

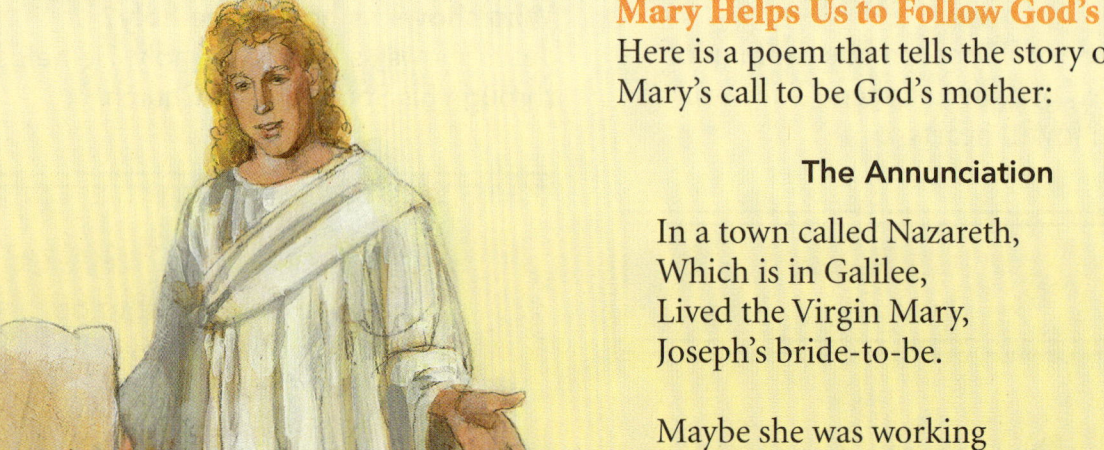

Mary Helps Us to Follow God's Call

Here is a poem that tells the story of Mary's call to be God's mother:

The Annunciation

In a town called Nazareth,
Which is in Galilee,
Lived the Virgin Mary,
Joseph's bride-to-be.

Maybe she was working
And humming happily, too,
The day the angel came and said,
"Hail, the Lord is with you."

"Do not be afraid, Mary.
You are a favored one.
God has chosen you to be
The mother of his Son."

Mary said to Gabriel,
"With joy I'll do God's will."
Jesus' mother she became,
God's promise to fulfill.

God's own mother, Mary blest,
You are our mother, too.
Pray for us, your children,
And make us just like you.

Mary answered God's call with "Yes, I will do as you wish." She called herself God's handmaid. She will help us do God's will also, if we ask her. Mary is the Mother of the Church, all those who believe in her Son.

- Who are messengers of God for you? What might they tell you to do?
- How can these boys and girls show that they have listened to God's messengers?

Color these words. We say them to God when we do what his messengers tell us.

YES, LORD

19

Mary Calls Us to Pray the Rosary

Mothers like to receive handmade gifts from their children. Sometimes children pick flowers and give them to their mothers.

Our mother Mary likes to receive a special garland, or crown of flowers, from us. This garland is the rosary. Its prayers are like a garland of roses. Over and over in the rosary we say the beautiful words of the Annunciation to Mary.

People have prayed a form of the rosary for hundreds of years. It is a powerful prayer that many Catholics love to pray.

Today our rosary has fifty Hail Marys in sets of ten (called decades). Each decade begins with an Our Father and ends with the Glory Be.

We pray the rosary not only with words but with our minds and hearts too. During each decade we think about a mystery. A mystery is an event in the life of Jesus, Mary, and the Church.

Number each set of mysteries from 1 to 5 in order. Why are the mysteries called joyful, luminous, sorrowful, and glorious?

Joyful Mysteries

_____ The Visitation

_____ The Presentation

_____ The Annunciation

_____ The Birth of Jesus

_____ The Finding of Jesus

Luminous Mysteries

_____ The Wedding Feast at Cana

_____ The Institution of the Eucharist

_____ Proclamation of the Kingdom

_____ Jesus' Baptism

_____ The Transfiguration

Sorrowful Mysteries

_____ The Death of Our Lord

_____ The Scourging

_____ The Crowning with Thorns

_____ The Agony in the Garden

_____ The Carrying of the Cross

Glorious Mysteries

_____ The Resurrection

_____ The Coming of the Holy Spirit

_____ The Crowning of Mary

_____ The Ascension

_____ The Assumption

Color the garland and think of the Annunciation.

The Church named October the month of the rosary and celebrates the Feast of the Holy Rosary on October 7. When we pray the rosary, we honor Mary and come to know and love her Son better. Our faith grows stronger. We receive blessings for ourselves and for the whole world.

We Remember

Why do Catholics pray the rosary?
Catholics pray the rosary to honor Mary and to know and love her Son Jesus more.

Words to Know
rosary   decade   mystery

We Respond

Hail Mary, full of grace,
the Lord is with you.

FAMILY CORNER

At the Annunciation, Mary was asked to be the mother of Jesus, God's Son. By saying yes, she became our spiritual mother, the Mother of the Church and of all people. We show our love for Mary by trying to answer God's calls willingly and promptly, as she did. We honor her in a special way by praying the rosary.

 Read
Luke 1:26–38

Discuss
- How did Mary answer God's call?
- How does God call us to do things for him?
- How can we answer God's call as Mary did?
- When did God call you today and how did you answer?

 Pray
Holy Mary, Mother of God, pray for us sinners, now and at the hour of our death.

Do
- Display Mary's picture or statue.
- Each evening pray the family rosary— or at least one decade.
- Make a rosary out of seeds, nuts, corn, cord, or flowers.
- Sing a song honoring Mary.
- Act out a mystery of the rosary and then pray that decade together.

_____

❏ Signature

21

5 We Are Called to Follow Jesus

Jesus Called Apostles

Jesus called some men to be his special followers. This is the story as Peter, the chief **apostle,** might tell it:

> My brother Andrew and I are fishermen. One day as we were casting our nets into the sea, Jesus passed by. He called, "Come after me, and I will make you fishers of men." We left our nets and followed him. A little way down the shore we saw James and John, who are brothers. They were in their boats mending nets with their father. Jesus called these brothers too, and they joined us.
>
> adapted from Mark 1:16–20

Later Jesus called eight other men to be his apostles—twelve in all. They came to believe that Jesus was the Son of God sent by the Father to save us. The apostles taught people the Good News. They healed the sick in Jesus' name. They became the first Church leaders.

How do these people say yes to their call to follow Jesus?

- your mother
- your father
- your teacher
- your parish priest
- a friend of yours
- you

Jesus Called Some People to Be His Disciples

Jesus also called seventy-two people to be his **disciples.** They were to help him bring all people to God our Father. Jesus looked at a field of ripe grain. He said, "The field is full of grain, but there are only a few workers. Pray that God will send workers to gather in the harvest."
adapted from Luke 10:1–2

Jesus still calls people to follow him today. He calls Christians to teach and live what he taught and to pray that more people become Christians. Jesus wants us to pray for more priests, deacons, brothers, and sisters to serve his Church. Then he will have many helpers to spread the Good News of God's love.

Jesus Called Saul to Be His Apostle
(A Play)

Cast Reader   Jesus   Ananias
Saul   Friends

Scene I

Reader: Saul, along with some friends, was on his way to Damascus. He was going to arrest disciples of Jesus. They would be put to death. Suddenly light from the sky flashed around Saul. He fell to the ground with his eyes closed. Then he heard a voice.

Jesus: Saul, Saul, why are you persecuting me?

Saul: Who are you, sir?

Jesus: I am Jesus, whom you are persecuting.

Saul: What am I to do, Lord?

Jesus: Get up. Go into the city. There you will be told what you must do.

(Jesus leaves. Saul stands and opens his eyes.)

Saul: I see nothing. The light has blinded me.

Reader: Saul was led away by his friends. They too had heard the voice but had seen no one.

Scene II

Reader: Later Jesus appeared to a disciple named Ananias.

Ananias: Here I am, Lord.

Jesus: Ananias, go to Straight Street. Find the man Saul who is praying and give him sight.

Ananias: Lord, that man hates Christians.

Jesus: It will be all right. I have chosen Saul to be my apostle.

(Ananias goes to Saul. He places his hands on Saul's head.)

Ananias: Brother Saul, the Lord has sent me. Receive your sight.

Saul: *(Stands up)* I can see!

Ananias: Jesus wants you to be filled with the Holy Spirit. It is time you were baptized and had your sins washed away. Call upon Jesus.

Saul: Jesus! Jesus!

Reader: Saul told many people about Jesus and brought them into the Church. He had to suffer much, but he suffered gladly because of his great love for Jesus. Saul became Paul.

adapted from Acts 9:1–22

A Secret Message from God

Find 33 squares this size: ☐ Color them black to see God's message.

God Calls Us to Be His

R __ TH

P __ T __ R

__ BR __ H __ M

M __ RY

__ P __ STL __ S

D __ V __ D

D __ SC __ PL __ S

G __ BR __ __ L

FR __ NC __ S

P __ __ L

__ S

D
_ N _ W
_ O _
P
S _ _ _
_ _ _ E
R

Fill the clouds with names of people called by God. To climb the mountain, put in words that tell how we respond to God's call. Use the Word Bank.

Word Bank

Abraham	love	apostles
Mary	David	Paul
know	Ruth	Peter
Francis	disciples	serve
Gabriel	us	care

Word Search

Find and circle 13 words that tell what Jesus' disciples do. The words go across and down.

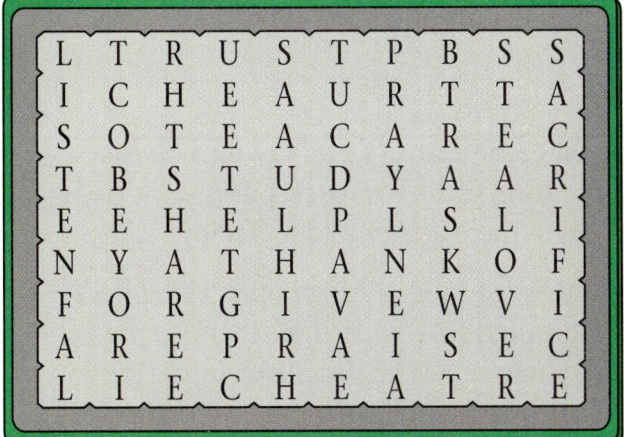

```
L T R U S T P B S S
I C H E A U R T T A
S O T E A C A R E C
T B S T U D Y A A R
E E H E L P S L I I
N Y A T H A N K O F
F O R G I V E W V I
A R E P R A I S E C
L I E C H E A T R E
```

Words to Know
apostle   disciple

We Remember

What does Jesus call Christians to help him do?
Jesus calls Christians to help him spread the Good News of God's love.

We Respond

What am I to do, Lord?

FAMILY CORNER

True disciples of Jesus listen to his words and walk in his way. They show their love for the Lord by sharing in his mission of leading all people to the Father.

 **Read**
Luke 10:1–2

Discuss
- What does Jesus ask us to do in this part of the Gospel?
- How do we show we are working for Jesus?
- What prayer will we say to ask God for more workers?

 **Pray**
What am I to do, Lord?

Do
- Make a prayer corner in your home to help you remember to pray for more workers for Jesus.
- Tell your child how a priest, deacon, brother, or sister helped you.
- Find out how many apostles each person in the family can name.
- Invite a priest, deacon, brother, or sister to your house for a family meal.
- Ask your child to tell the story about Jesus' calling of Saul to be his apostle.

❏ Signature

We Are God's Holy People

(Have the children write their names on one side of a card and the name of any person of faith on the other side.)

Leader 1: God called Abraham to believe that Abraham's family would be his people. God called David to serve him and his chosen people. God called Mary, a woman of faith, to be the Mother of the Savior.

Leader 2: Jesus called Peter and the other apostles to lead his people. He called disciples to carry on his work. He called Paul to bring others to the faith. God calls us at Baptism. We belong to the people of faith. We are Catholic Christians who follow Jesus.

Reader: A reading from Paul's letter to the Ephesians:

You are fellow citizens with the holy ones and members of the household of God, built upon the foundation of the apostles and prophets, with Christ Jesus himself as the capstone. Through him the whole structure is held together and grows into a temple sacred in the Lord.

Ephesians 2:19–21

Leader 1: Let us build a structure to show how we form the Church with all the holy people of God. As you place your card, read the names on it and say, "... belong to God's holy people."

(Children go up and stand cards folded in half next to each other. Unfolded cards laid on these can support other levels.)

Side 1: God, we believe in you. We trust you.

Side 2: Jesus, we follow you. Deepen our love.

Side 1: Holy Spirit, strengthen our faith.

Side 2: Mary, Mother of the Church, pray for us.

Leader 2: Let us listen to God and pray in our hearts.

(Pass around box of verses from Master 10. Each child draws one out. All pray silently. End with a song.)

FAMILY FEATURE

Honoring Mary, Mother of God

The Sidoni family lives in a section of Cleveland, Ohio, known as Little Italy. A high point of the year for their parish, Holy Rosary, is the feast of the Assumption, August 15, when the Church celebrates Mary being taken body and soul to heaven. The Sidonis even named their daughter Assumpta. Each year the Italian-Americans begin the four-day feast with Mass. Then in a procession led by the cross, the statue of Mary is transported on a float covered with flowers. People watching the procession put money on the statue for the use of the parish and for the poor. Through the neighborhood streets the people walk, praying litanies and singing hymns. Fireworks are shot off. Then the statue is brought to a special shrine. At the end of the four days there is another procession and the statue is returned to church.

In some Italian parishes the procession concludes with the statue of Mary meeting a float carrying the statue of Jesus. Both proceed to the church, symbolizing Mary's entrance into eternal glory with her Son. The ceremony concludes with benediction of the Blessed Sacrament.

In other countries on this day Mary's statue is decorated differently. In the Philippines it is put on a platform on a boat decorated with flowers and is taken to nearby towns. In some countries the feast is a harvest festival, and the statue of Mary is decorated with sheaves of ripe grain. In France, whose patron saint is Mary under the title of the Assumption, her statue is surrounded by wine grapes.

All Catholics honor Mary, the Mother of the Church, especially on her feasts. In your home each evening, you might pray the family rosary, or at least a decade. An interesting family project is to make a rosary using unique items for beads, such as acorns or pieces of Styrofoam. You might also display a picture or statue of Mary in an obvious place and decorate it with flowers and candles on feasts such as the following:

August 15
Assumption

August 22
Queenship of the Virgin Mary

September 8
Birth of the Virgin Mary

October 7
Our Lady of the Rosary

November 21
Presentation of the Virgin Mary

December 8
Immaculate Conception

December 12
Our Lady of Guadalupe

January 1
Solemnity of Mary, Mother of God

March 25
Annunciation of the Lord

Saturday following the Second Sunday after Pentecost
Immaculate Heart of Mary

May 31
Visitation

July 16
Our Lady of Mount Carmel

Christians

Play "Following Jesus." One person begins by saying, "I'm following Jesus and I'm bringing (name of something a Christian should have, such as a Bible or a loving heart)." The next person repeats what the first person says and adds something. The game continues until someone can no longer repeat the list in order.

Good News!

Find the messages in the Good News notes by using the code.

(Answers: Christ saved us. Jesus died and rose. We can live forever. God loves us.)

UNIT 2

Jesus Is with Us on Our Way

The sacraments are signs of the special presence and sanctifying action of Jesus among his people, the Church. In this unit the children deepen their knowledge of the sacraments, especially Baptism, the Eucharist, and Reconciliation (Penance). Their faith is strengthened as they gain a better understanding of the effects of the sacraments on themselves and on the whole family of God. They are motivated to frequent celebration of the sacraments of Reconciliation and Holy Eucharist. And they are guided to participate in Mass with greater understanding, eagerness, and love.

6 God Shares the Wondrous Life of Grace

Jesus Brings Us a Share in God's Life

God loved the first people he made very much. He wanted them to enjoy a close friendship with him. So God shared his own life, or **grace,** with them. He made them like God so that they belonged to his family. They could live forever.

But Adam and Eve had the power to choose. They refused God's friendship. They chose to disobey God. They were selfish and sinned. They lost grace and were no longer God's children.

Adam and Eve's sin brought something new into the world. Because of this first sin, people now are born without grace. We tend to be selfish and not love God. This is what it means to be born in **original sin.**

Adam and Eve were sorry for what they had done. God's love for us was so great that he sent his own Son, Jesus, to save us from sin and death. Because Jesus died and rose for us, we can share in God's life again. We can belong to God's family as his children. We can live with God forever in heaven.

Word Choice

Underline the word or phrase that completes each sentence.

1. God gave his life to Adam and Eve so that they would (be his children, be as great as he is, not obey him).

2. Our share in God's life is called (love, grace, hope).

3. God sent (Adam and Eve, Mary, Jesus) to save us from sin and death.

4. We are born in original sin, which means without (sight, speech, the life of grace).

We Receive the Life of Grace in Baptism

An important man named Nicodemus came to Jesus and said, "We know that you are a teacher from God. No one else can do the things you do. God is with you."

Jesus told him, "You must be born of water and the Spirit to enter God's kingdom."

"How can that be?" Nicodemus asked. Jesus was talking about **Baptism.** Through his death on the cross and his rising, Jesus gives God's life in Baptism to those who believe in him. The Bible says,

> God so loved the world that he gave his only Son, so that everyone who believes in him may have eternal life.
> adapted from John 3:16

Most of us were baptized as babies. Our parents and godparents took us to church. They promised to help us live as Christians.

Then the priest or deacon baptized us with water. He called us by name and said, "I baptize you in the name of the Father, and of the Son, and of the Holy Spirit."

These words and the water are the signs in the Sacrament of Baptism. When they are used, we join in the death and rising of Jesus. God gives us grace, takes away original sin, and forgives our sins. In Baptism we tell God that we want to keep away from sin and follow his Son. We become God's children and are welcomed into God's family, the Church.

A Puzzle on Baptism

Fill in the missing words in the acrostic puzzle. The sentences and the Word Bank will help you.

1. In Baptism we share in God's life called _____ .

2. _____ is poured on us when we are baptized.

3. The grace we receive in Baptism is new _____ .

4. _____ told us that we can live with him if we are baptized.

5. Through Baptism we become members of the Church, God's _____ .

Word Bank
water   family   life
grace   Jesus

We Are Headed for Heaven

What is heaven like? St. Paul answers that question in the Bible:

> No one has ever seen or heard anything like it! No one can imagine what wonderful things God has prepared for those who love him.
> adapted from 1 Corinthians 2:9

Living the Life of Grace

Start with the letter *P* at the bottom of the puzzle path. Circle every second letter to find the words that complete the sentences. They will tell you how to live your life of grace and grow as a child of God.

1. _____ every day.

2. Listen when the _____ is read. Try to read from it yourself.

3. Receive Jesus in Holy _____ .

4. Obey God's _____ .

5. _____ the gifts God has given you.

All of the **sacraments** are special ways in which God shares his life with us.

Match the name of a sacrament (Baptism, Reconciliation, Eucharist) with each picture here.

_____

_____

_____

Words to Know
grace Baptism
original sin sacraments

We Remember

What does Baptism do for us?
Baptism gives us new life in Jesus. We become members of the Church and children of God.

We Respond

You will show me the path to life, fullness of joys forever.
adapted from Psalm 16:11

FAMILY CORNER

Out of great love for us, God sent his only Son to suffer and die so that we could share in his life. This life of grace was given to us in Baptism. Through this sacrament God dwells in us and enables us to live as his children. We can grow in grace through prayer, the sacraments, and trying to lead a good Christian life.

Read
John 3:1–17

Discuss
- What kind of man was Nicodemus?
- How did Jesus describe Baptism?
- Why is water such a meaningful sign of Baptism? (Consider some uses of water.)
- How did Jesus earn the grace we receive in Baptism?

Pray
As a deer longs for running water, so my soul longs for you, O God.
adapted from Psalm 42:2

Do
- Have a baptismal anniversary celebration for each member of the family.
- Light the baptismal candle and have all members of the family renew their baptismal promises.
- If someone you know will soon be baptized, make the white robe or provide the candle.
- Talk about how you as a family are living your life of grace. Refer to page 33.

_____
❏ Signature

7 The Holy Spirit Lives within Us

The Two Great Laws
Unscramble these words and fill in the blanks.

1. VOEL
2. DGO
3. SHOETR

Jesus Is the Way to Eternal Life
Once a rich young man asked Jesus, "What must I do to have eternal life?"

Jesus said, "Keep the commandments."

The man told Jesus, "I have kept all these since I was a boy."

Then Jesus answered,

> "If you want to show your love, go and sell all you have. Give the money to the poor. Then come and follow me. You will have treasure in heaven."
>
> adapted from Mark 10:17–21

Write, in the chest, the words from the list for four of heaven's treasures.

fun   angels   friends
beauty   peace   Mary
God   joy

35

The Holy Spirit Leads Us to Do Good

It is sometimes hard to follow Jesus, so Jesus sent us a helper.

The Holy Spirit has lived within us since our Baptism. The Spirit makes us more like Jesus. St. Paul tells us:

> Like mirrors we reflect the brightness of the Lord. We grow brighter and brighter as we are changed into the image of Jesus. This is the work of the Holy Spirit.
> adapted from 2 Corinthians 3:18

The Holy Spirit shares with us his own goodness and leads us to heaven.

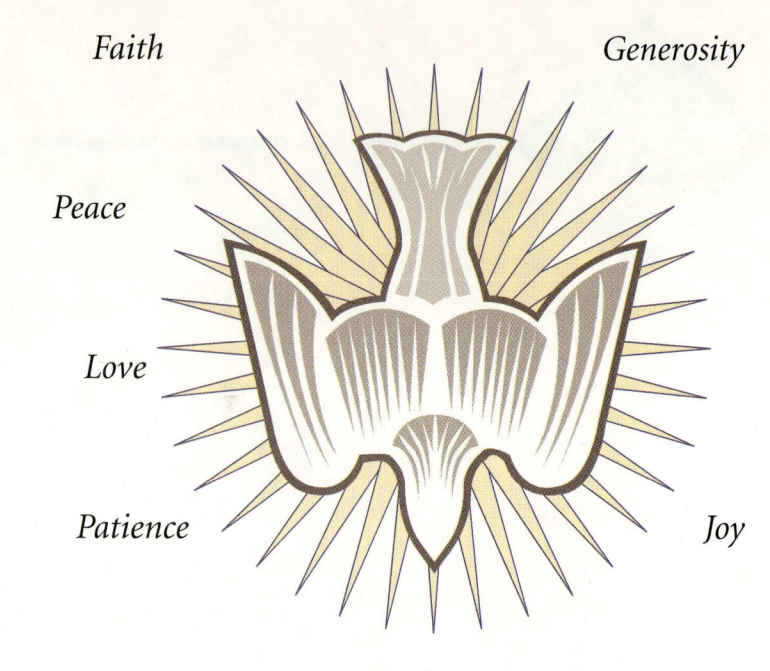

Faith   *Generosity*

Peace

Love

Patience   *Joy*

Kindness

The words around the dove tell some good things the Holy Spirit shares.

36

Choose a picture. Write a story about it. Tell how the Spirit brings one of these good things into someone's life.

Come, Holy Spirit, fill the hearts of your faithful, and kindle in them the fire of your love.

My Story

_____

_____

_____

_____

_____

The Holy Spirit Helps Us Avoid Evil

With the Spirit's help we can overcome temptations and avoid sin. St. Paul says:

> If you let the Holy Spirit lead you, you will not be selfish.
> People who are selfish make enemies. They fight and argue. They hurt themselves and others.
>
> If the Spirit leads you, you will be full of love, joy, peace, kindness, and goodness. Since the Spirit has given us life, let us also follow the Spirit.
>
> adapted from Galatians 5:16, 19, 25

The Holy Spirit helps us to be truly wise. To be wise means to know what is good and what is evil. If we listen to the Holy Spirit, we will know what is right. We will be able to say no to temptation and sin. We will be able to do what is good.

The Holy Spirit gives us special help when we pray and celebrate the sacraments.

Color all the roads the Spirit would tell you to take from Old Town to New Town.

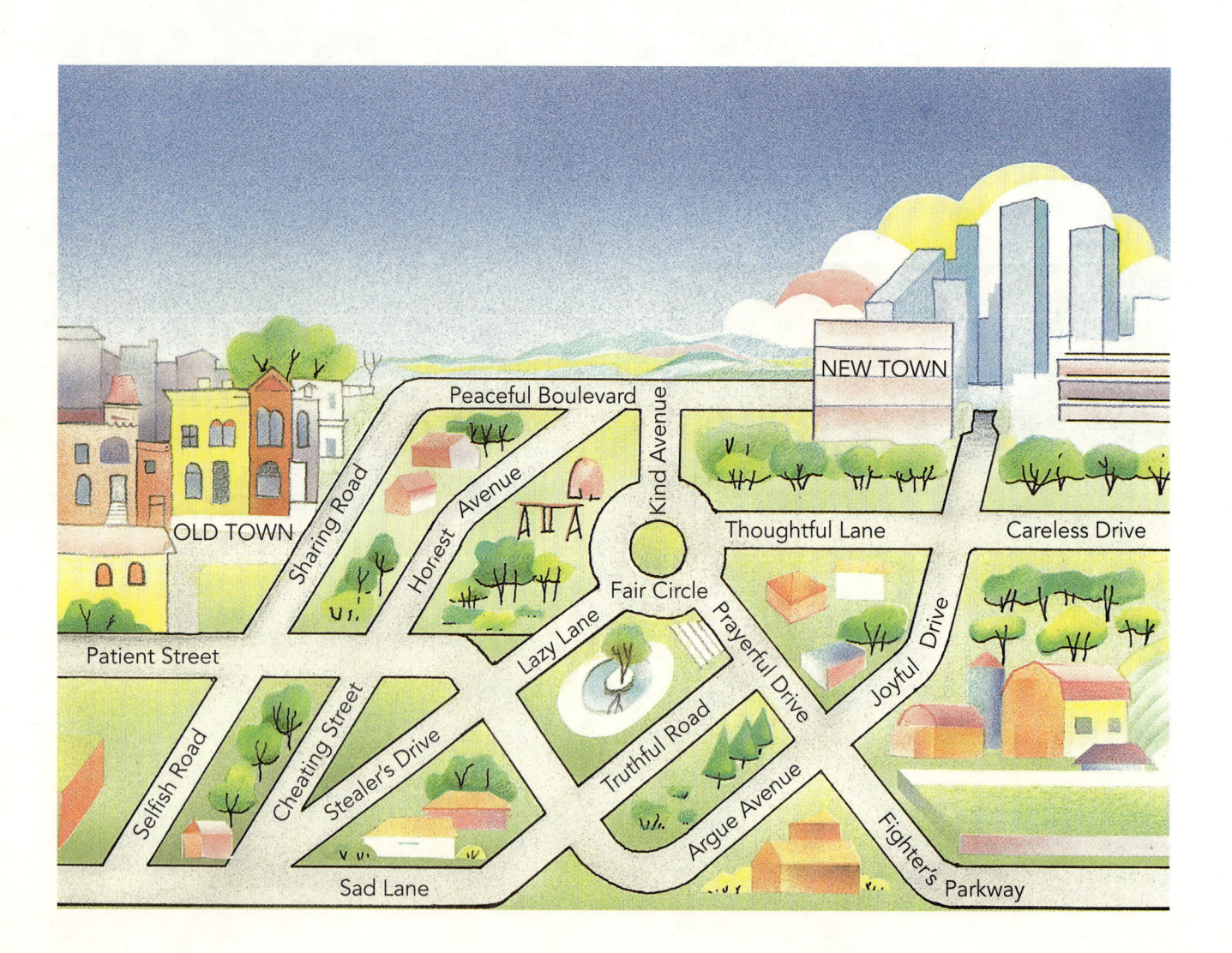

Complete the sentence beside each picture. Use the Word Bank.

The Holy Spirit helps us know what is good when we _____.

The Holy Spirit fills us with grace when we receive Holy _____.

The Holy Spirit helps us say no to sin when we celebrate the Sacrament of _____.

Word Bank
Reconciliation
Communion
pray

We Remember

What is sin?
Sin is choosing to think, say, or do what we know offends God and what may also hurt ourselves and others.

We Respond

Come, Holy Spirit, fill the hearts of your faithful, and kindle in them the fire of your love.

FAMILY CORNER

The Holy Spirit helps us, through his gifts, to do good and avoid evil. He leads us to reflect the image of the Lord, according to our gifts, until we are changed into the image of Jesus. This is the will of God—our sanctification.

Read
2 Corinthians 3:18

Discuss
- What is meant by the "brightness" of Jesus?
- In what ways can we reflect his "brightness"?
- How can we cooperate with the Holy Spirit?
- How can we help one another reflect the goodness of Jesus?

Pray
Holy Spirit, make me like Jesus.

Do
- Act out situations that provide an opportunity for following the Holy Spirit.
- Plan to read about Jesus' life in the Gospels. You may do this as a family a few minutes a day or on a certain day of the week before the evening meal, perhaps.
- Ask your child to tell the story of St. Dominic Savio.

_____

❏ Signature

8 God Blesses Contrite Hearts

Jesus Forgave Peter

At the Last Supper Jesus said to Peter, "Simon, the devil will tempt you, but I have prayed that your faith will not fail." Peter loved Jesus and promised, "Lord, I will go to prison and die with you."

Jesus knew that Peter was weak. He warned, "Before the rooster crows today, you will deny three times that you know me."

After the supper Jesus and the apostles went to a garden. There Jesus said, "Pray that you will not be tempted." Then he went to pray to his Father. When he came back, the apostles were asleep. "Why are you sleeping?" Jesus asked. "Get up and pray."

As Jesus spoke, a crowd came to arrest him. They took him away to judge him. Peter followed.

A girl saw Peter and said, "This man too was with Jesus." Peter said, "I do not know him."

After a while a man noticed Peter and said, "You are one of his friends." But Peter answered, "My friend, I am not!"

Later another man said of Peter, "Surely this man was with Jesus. He is a Galilean." Peter said, "I do not know what you are talking about."

While he was saying this, the rooster crowed. Just then, Jesus turned and looked at Peter. Peter remembered the Lord's words and went out and wept.

Jesus, who loved Peter, knew his sorrow and forgave him. He made Peter head of his Church.

adapted from Luke 22:31–62

Sin offends God, who is good and loving. It hurts all the members of the Church. Sin sets us apart from God's holy people. When we see our sins and we are sorry, we ask forgiveness.

Write the parts of the Act of Contrition that answer the questions.

1. How sorry are you?

_____

2. In what two ways have you sinned?

_____

_____

3. Against whom have you sinned?

_____

_____

4. What three things do you promise to do?

_____

_____

5. In whose name do you ask forgiveness?

_____

Act of Contrition

My God,
I am sorry for my sins with
all my heart.
In choosing to do wrong
and failing to do good,
I have sinned against you
whom I should love above
all things.
I firmly intend, with your
help,
to do penance,
to sin no more,
and to avoid
whatever leads me to sin.
Our Savior Jesus Christ
suffered and died for us.
In his name, my God, have
mercy.

God's Word Tells of His Forgiving Love

Do you remember these Bible stories? What do they teach about God and sinners?

The Two Men in the Temple

Two men went up to the Temple to pray. The first man thought of the good things he had done and prayed: "O God, I thank you that I am not like other people—greedy, dishonest, and unkind. I thank you that I am better than this tax collector."

The other man stayed far back and bowed his head. He thought of the times he had not kept all of God's commandments. He said, "O God, be merciful to me, a sinner." God was pleased with the second man because he was sorry. This man went home with God's peace, but the other did not.

adapted from Luke 18:10–14

Jesus and the Sinful Woman

One day a man named Simon invited Jesus to his house for a meal. While Jesus and the other guests were eating, a woman came into the room. She was sad because she had not always kept God's laws of love. She came to tell Jesus she was sorry.

The sinful woman went straight to Jesus. She washed his feet with her tears. She wiped them with her long hair and anointed them with perfumed oil. Jesus looked at her with love. He was pleased that she was sorry.

Simon did not like this. He thought Jesus should not let a sinner touch him. Jesus knew what Simon was thinking and said, "This woman's many sins have been forgiven, so she has shown great love."

Then Jesus spoke to the woman and said: "Your sins are forgiven. Go in peace." The woman's heart was filled with peace and joy.

adapted from Luke 7:36–50

The Shepherd and His Lost Sheep

A man had a hundred sheep. One ran away and got lost. The shepherd loved the lost sheep just as he loved all the sheep in his flock. Because he knew the others were all right, he left the ninety-nine and went to look for the lost one. He searched everywhere until he found it. Then he lifted it up on his shoulders and with great joy carried it back.

When he got home, he invited his friends and neighbors to celebrate. He said, "Rejoice with me because I have found my lost sheep." In the same way, there is great joy in heaven whenever a sinner is sorry.

adapted from Luke 15:4–7

Jesus and Zacchaeus

One day Jesus was passing through the town of Jericho. A rich tax collector named Zacchaeus, who was very short, climbed a tree to see Jesus. When Jesus saw him, he said, "Zacchaeus, come down quickly, for I must stay at your house today."

Zacchaeus hurried down and welcomed Jesus with joy. Some people began to grumble, "Jesus has gone to the house of a sinner."

But Zacchaeus was sorry for cheating the people. He told Jesus, "I will give half of my belongings to the poor. If I have cheated anyone, I will pay back four times as much."

Jesus was pleased and said, "The blessing of God has come to this house today."

adapted from Luke 19:1–10

Do We Have a Disciple's Heart?

The Holy Spirit helps us examine our consciences to see how we have kept God's laws. When we admit and are sorry for our sins, God gives us peace. Daily **examination of conscience** helps us root out ugly things in our heart. We become more loving disciples of Jesus.

Examination of Conscience

1. Have I prayed attentively to God each morning and evening?
2. Have I always used God's name with love and respect?
3. Have I celebrated Sundays and holy days with Mass? How well have I prayed and sung?
4. Have I obeyed my parents and others in authority? How have I shown them love and respect?
5. How have I cared for the gift of life—my health and that of others? Do I show respect for my body and the bodies of others?
6. Have I used my gifts to serve God and others? How kind have I been to my family? to other children? to the poor, the old, and the handicapped?
7. How well have I cared for the gifts of God? Have I shared with those in need?
8. Have I spoken the truth? kept secrets and promises? been kind? spoken up for what is right?

We Remember

When does God forgive us?
God forgives us when we are sorry for our sins.

Words to Know
examination of conscience

Words to Memorize
Act of Contrition

We Respond

I am sorry for my sins with all my heart.

FAMILY CORNER

No matter what our sins, Jesus is always ready to reconcile us with himself and the Father if we are sorry. We need but to trust in him and allow his love to help us change our lives.

Read
Luke 7:36–50

Discuss
- How did the sinful woman show love?
- What did Jesus say to teach that the more we are forgiven, the more we love?
- Why did Jesus forgive the woman?

Pray
Thank you, Jesus, for your forgiving love.

Do
- Discuss symbols of sorrow, peace, and reconciliation. Use them on a banner.
- Hang a crucifix or picture of Jesus in your home as a sign of God's presence.

❏ Signature

God Forgives Us in the Sacrament of Reconciliation

9

A Father Forgives His Son

Jesus told this story about a father and son.

Reader: Once there was a rich man who had two sons. One day the younger son came to his father and said . . .

Son: Father, give me my share of the money. I am tired of living at home. I want to see some new things.

Father: I am sorry that you want to leave home, but here is the money.

Reader: The son was happy at first. He wasted his money having good times with his friends. When the money ran out, his friends left him. He had to find work because he had nothing to eat. The only job he could get was feeding pigs. Even then he was hungry most of the time. One day he sat down to think about what he had done.

Son: What have I done? I have hurt my father. I have hurt myself. Even the pigs have more food than I do.

Reader: Then the son began to feel sorry for the way he had behaved.

Son: I am so sorry that I hurt my father. He worked so hard for that money.

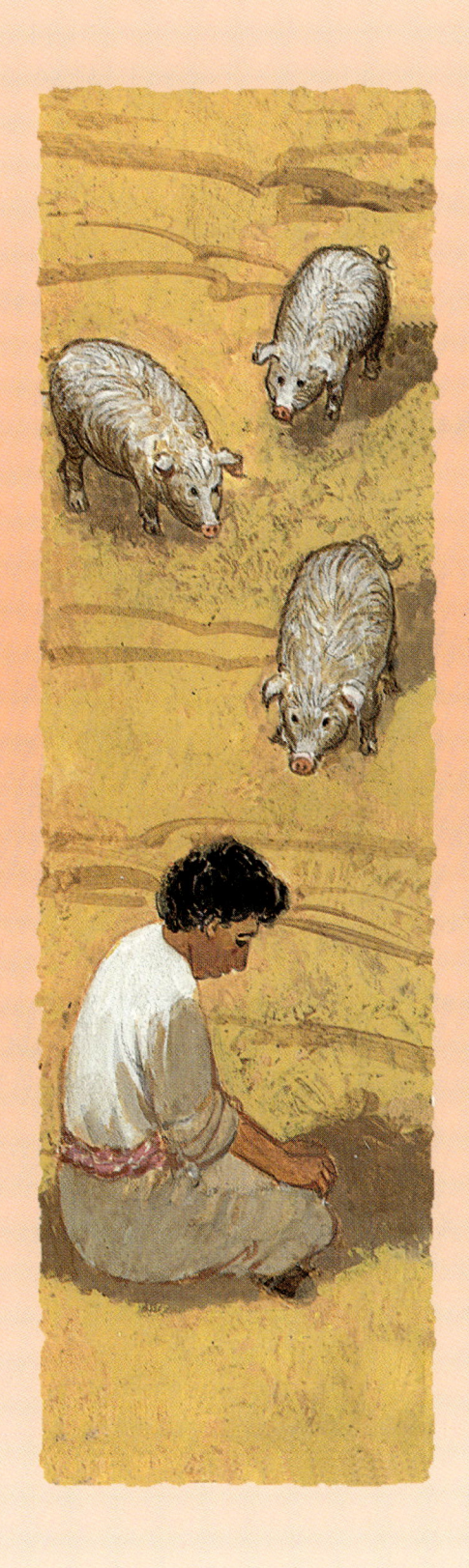

Reader: The young man tried to decide what he should do about it.

Son: I know what I will do. I will go back to my father. I will never be so selfish again. I will try to please my father.

Reader: The son tried to think of what to say to his father.

Son: I will tell my father what I have done and that I am sorry.

Reader: The young man wanted to do something to make up to his father for what he had done.

Son: I will do anything he wants. I will work as a servant in his house.

Reader: The son went home. When he was still a long way off, his father saw him coming. He ran to meet his son. The father put his arms around him and welcomed him.

Son: Father, I am sorry.

Father: Welcome home, my son. You are forgiven. Servants, bring him the finest robe, a ring, and sandals. Come, we must celebrate!

adapted from Luke 15:11–24

Like the son in the story, we ask our Father's forgiveness when we celebrate the Sacrament of Reconciliation or Penance.

Draw a picture of yourself in the white box telling God that you are sorry.

We Prepare for the Sacrament of Reconciliation

Jesus loves us, even when we fail to love him and others. He forgives our sins when we are sorry. He forgives us in the Sacrament of Reconciliation.

- ✤ I ask the Holy Spirit to help me celebrate this sacrament. Come, Holy Spirit, help me look into my heart. Show me where I have failed to love God and others. Help me to be sorry. Help me to grow in God's life. Amen.
- ✤ I examine my conscience to find out how I have sinned in my thoughts, my words, my actions, or what I have failed to do.
- ✤ I pray an Act of Contrition to tell God that I am sorry.
- ✤ I promise to be better.
- ✤ I ask God to help me love him and others more.

Ten Steps to Forgiveness

When I celebrate the Sacrament of Reconciliation, I meet Jesus. I meet him through the priest who hears my confession.

1. The priest welcomes me. I greet him.

2. I make the Sign of the Cross and say how long it has been since my last confession.

3. I listen to the priest's prayer and Scripture reading.

4. I confess my sins. I may tell the priest any problems I face in living as a Catholic and may ask questions.

5. I listen to the priest. Then he gives me a penance.

6. I pray an Act of Contrition.

7. When the priest gives me absolution, I make the Sign of the Cross.

8. The priest may say, "Give thanks to the Lord, for he is good." I answer, "His mercy endures forever."

9. The priest may say something like "Good-bye. God loves you." I say, "Thank you, Father," and I leave.

10. I thank God for his forgiving love and peace. I ask the Holy Spirit to help me live as God's loving child. I do the penance the priest has given me. If it is a prayer, I pray it right away. If it is a deed, I do it as soon as I can.

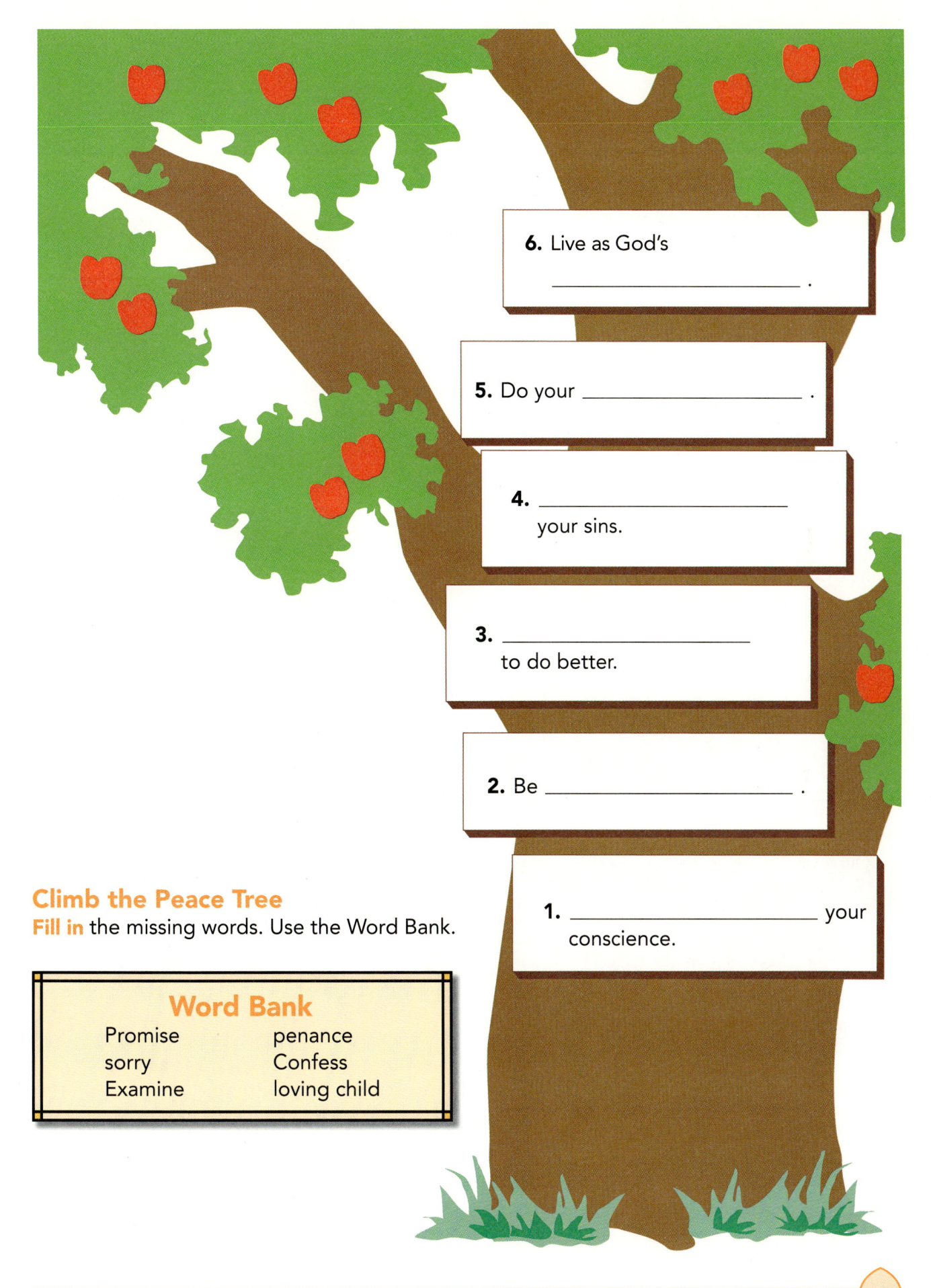

6. Live as God's _____ .

5. Do your _____ .

4. _____ your sins.

3. _____ to do better.

2. Be _____ .

1. _____ your conscience.

Climb the Peace Tree
Fill in the missing words. Use the Word Bank.

Word Bank
Promise   penance
sorry   Confess
Examine   loving child

49

Jesus Forgives Us

Print the missing words in the squares to finish the Peace Flag. Use the Word Bank.

P Jesus gave the apostles and _____ power to forgive sins.

E When we tell our sins to the priest, we _____ them.

A When we carefully look over what we have done, we _____ our conscience.

C Jesus loves _____ hearts.

E The priest gives us a _____ to make up for our sins and to turn us away from them.

Word Bank
confess   penance   contrite
examine   priests

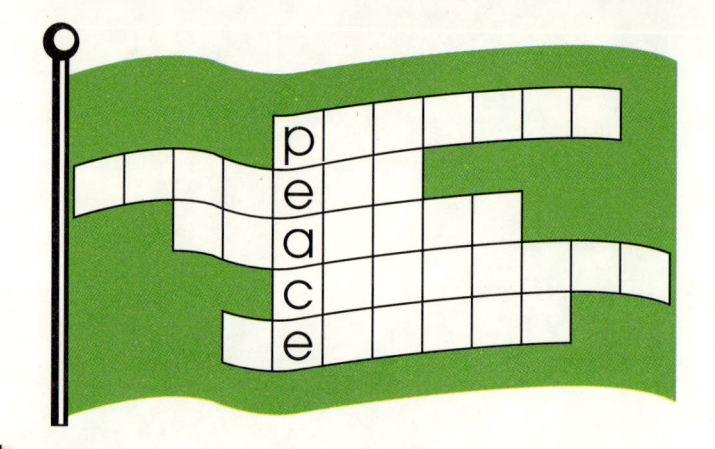

We Remember

What does Jesus do for us in the Sacrament of Reconciliation?
Jesus forgives us and gives us his peace and love in the Sacrament of Reconciliation.

We Respond

Give thanks to the LORD, who is good, whose love endures forever.

Psalm 118:1

FAMILY CORNER

Our loving, forgiving Father always welcomes us when we return to him, after we sin, in the Sacrament of Reconciliation. In celebrating the sacrament, we express sorrow for our offenses and trust in God's mercy.

Read
Luke 15:11–32

Discuss
- How are the five steps for receiving the Sacrament of Reconciliation shown in the story of the Forgiving Father?
- How is the father in the story like God, our heavenly Father?
- What can we do when we feel unforgiving toward others?

Pray
O God, have mercy on me, a sinner.

Do
- Conduct a family reconciliation service.
- Make a "paper movie" of the forgiving father and the lost son. (Draw pictures on a roll of shelf paper or similar material. Tell the story while you show the pictures.)
- Decide on steps to renew some broken or forgotten friendships.

❏ Signature

10 God's Family Celebrates the Eucharist

The Mass Is a Meal in Memory of Jesus

Families share meals together. God's family shares a special meal together. The **Eucharistic celebration** or **Mass** is the special family meal of the Church. It is our best way to give praise and thanks to God. Catholics celebrate Sunday by taking part in Mass. They celebrate special occasions with the Eucharist.

Jesus celebrated the first Mass when he had a special meal with his friends before he died. At Jesus' Last Supper, he took bread and said:

> "Take this, all of you, and eat it: this is my body, which will be given up for you."
>
> *from Eucharistic Prayer 1*

Then Jesus took the cup filled with wine. He thanked his Father, gave the apostles the cup, and said:

> "Take this, all of you, and drink from it: this is the cup of my blood. It will be shed for you and for all so that sins may be forgiven."
>
> *from Eucharistic Prayer 1*

Jesus shared himself as food and drink with his apostles. He told them, "Do this in memory of me." From that time on, through his apostles and priests, Jesus has made himself present in the Eucharist. When Jesus becomes present in the bread and wine, we can share in his death and resurrection.

The Mass Is a Sacrifice of Love

At every celebration of the Mass, Jesus shows his great love.

- He teaches us through the readings.
- He offers himself to God the Father for us.
- He makes us one with him and one with God's family in Holy Communion.
- He helps us to become more like him so that we can bring his love into the world.
- He strengthens us to continue his work.

All over the world Catholics celebrate the Eucharist. They remember Jesus and join in his sacrifice. They are united with him and one another.

52

Jesus Remains with Us

Jesus stays with us in our churches. We can visit him and speak with him when we wish. Those who are sick and dying can receive Communion at any time.

Sometimes we hold a special prayer service to honor Jesus in the Eucharist. The priest gives us the blessing of Jesus with the Sacred Host. We call this blessing **Benediction.** We bless ourselves by making the Sign of the Cross.

Complete the sentences. Use the Word Bank.

> **Word Bank**
> one another   Benediction   ~~Mass~~
> ~~Last Supper~~   ~~Holy Communion~~

1. We offer the sacrifice of Jesus at

   mass.

2. Jesus gave us the Eucharist at the

   Last Supper.

3. We receive Jesus as food and drink in

   Holy communion.

4. At Mass we become one with Jesus and

   with _one another_.

5. In a special prayer service we honor Jesus and receive his blessing called

   Benediction.

Jesus Speaks to Us at Mass

When Jesus lived on earth, he taught people the good news of salvation. One day Jesus went up a mountain and sat down to teach. The crowds listened to his words about his Father's love and how to live, but Jesus wanted them to put his words into practice too. So he ended with this story about two men who built houses.

"The first man built a house on rock. The rain fell, the floods came, and the winds blew hard against it. No harm was done to the house because it was built on rock. It was firm and strong. How wise the first man was to build his house on rock! The second man built a house on sand. The rain fell, the floods came, and the winds blew. His house fell and was completely ruined. How foolish the second man was to build his house on sand!"

Jesus explained the story:

> "Everyone who listens to my words and follows them will be like the wise man who built his house on rock. Everyone who listens to my words and does not follow them will be like the fool who built his house on sand."
> adapted from Matthew 7:24–27

54

When God's family celebrates the Eucharist, Jesus is present. He is present in the priest, his people, his Word, and the sacred Bread and Wine. He is present during the two main parts of the Mass: the Liturgy of the Word and the Liturgy of the Eucharist.

The **Liturgy of the Word** is the celebration of God's speaking to us. God himself teaches us through his words in the Bible.

A lector (reader) does the first reading. We listen and say, "Thanks be to God." Then we pray a psalm. In Sunday Masses and on feast days, there is a second reading.

To welcome the Gospel we stand and sing, "Alleluia." To show that Jesus speaks to us, we say, "Glory to you, Lord," as we make a cross on our foreheads, lips, and hearts.

We listen with our minds and hearts as the priest or deacon reads from the Gospel of Matthew, Mark, Luke, or John. Then we say, "Praise to you, Lord Jesus Christ."

A priest or deacon explains God's words in the homily. He tells how to live them. When we keep God's words, we are like the wise man who built his house on rock.

Circle five parts of the Liturgy of the Word that are God's Word to us.

We Respond

The promises of the LORD
I will sing forever.
Psalm 89:2

We Remember

Why did Jesus give us the Eucharist?
Jesus gave us the Eucharist so that we could join in his sacrifice to the Father and he could be with us as our spiritual food.

When does God speak to us at Mass?
God speaks to us in the Scripture readings and the homily during the Liturgy of the Word.

Words to Know
Eucharist   homily   Benediction
Gospel   Liturgy of the Word

FAMILY CORNER

The great love of Jesus is shown by his institution of the Holy Eucharist at the Last Supper. The sacrifice he offered for us through his death on the cross is renewed daily in the Mass. By participating in the Eucharist and making visits to the Blessed Sacrament, we grow in love for him and one another.

Read
Matthew 26:26–29

Discuss
- Why did Jesus give us himself in the Holy Eucharist?
- Why did Jesus suffer and die for us?
- How does the Mass help us remember Jesus' sacrifice?
- How can we give thanks to Jesus for the Holy Eucharist?

Pray
O Sacrament most holy,
O Sacrament divine,
All praise and all thanksgiving
Be every moment thine.

Do
- Make a family mobile of symbols of the Eucharist.
- Prepare for Sunday Mass as a family. Read and discuss the Scripture readings if possible. Decide how best to participate at Mass and prepare to receive Jesus.
- Have each member of the family write a short prayer thanking Jesus for his presence in the Holy Eucharist. Share the prayers in a little thanksgiving celebration or as part of grace after meals.
- Make a visit to church to thank Jesus for being with us in the Blessed Sacrament.

❏ Signature

11 The Eucharist Is a Gift

Gifts Show Love

Gifts speak. They say, "See, I love you!" The giver is loved more than the gift. Gifts help us grow in love, too. We love more after we have given or received a gift.

God gives gifts to show us love. He has given us the beautiful world. We take his gifts of wheat and grapes and, through our work, change them into bread and wine. They are signs of ourselves. Then at Mass we bring these as gifts to God. God's family gives God what we are and what we make.

We Offer Our Gifts with Jesus

God gives gifts to us too at Mass. In the Liturgy of the Word, he gives us the gift of his words. God tells us how much he loves us and how to live as his loving children. In the Liturgy of the Eucharist God gives us the gift of Holy Communion.

Jesus gave himself as a perfect gift to his Father. He did everything to please God. He died on the cross to save us from sin. Jesus offers the gift of his sacrifice on the cross for all people at every Mass.

The **Liturgy of the Eucharist** is a special gift exchange. The priest takes our gifts of bread and wine and offers them to God. During the Mass the bread and wine become Jesus.

Then, with Jesus, we offer Jesus and ourselves to God the Father. We do this in the Eucharistic Prayer, especially when the priest says:

"Through him, with him, in him,
in the unity of the Holy Spirit,
all honor and glory is yours,
almighty Father, forever and ever."

We respond to this prayer by saying "Amen" with great joy.

Then God gives us Jesus in Holy Communion as a gift of his love.

Print on each line the letter of the answer from the Word Bank.

Word Bank
A. God the Father
B. Jesus
C. his words
D. ourselves
E. love

_____ 1. What do all gifts show?

_____ 2. To whom do we offer gifts at Mass?

_____ 3. Who do our gifts of bread and wine become during Mass?

_____ 4. To whom did Jesus give the gift of himself when he died on the cross?

_____ 5. What gift does God give us in the Liturgy of the Word?

_____ 6. What gift do we receive in the Liturgy of the Eucharist?

_____ 7. At Mass what two gifts do we offer to God with Jesus?

At Mass we remember the dying and rising of Jesus. Jesus offers himself to the Father. We offer ourselves with him. We bring our prayers. We bring our joys and our sufferings. We bring all the good things we have done.

Jesus Makes Us One in Him

When Jesus gives himself to us as food and drink in the Holy Eucharist, we become one with him and his family, the Church. We are united with the Father and the Holy Spirit. We are united with Mary and all the angels and saints in heaven. We are united with everyone who shares the Eucharist on earth.

In a letter St. Paul reminds us that Jesus makes us one in Holy Communion:

> Though we are many, we are one body because we all share in the one bread which is Jesus.
> adapted from 1 Corinthians 10:17

In Holy Communion we come alive with the glorious life of Jesus. We become more like him. With his grace we can become better persons. Then, each time we take part in Mass, we can offer God a better gift.

Jesus Gives Us His Peace at Mass

During Mass God fills us with his life and love. God can use us then to bring his love and care to others. At the end of the Mass, the priest or deacon tells us, "Go in peace to love and serve the Lord."

We go out to share Christ's peace by loving others.

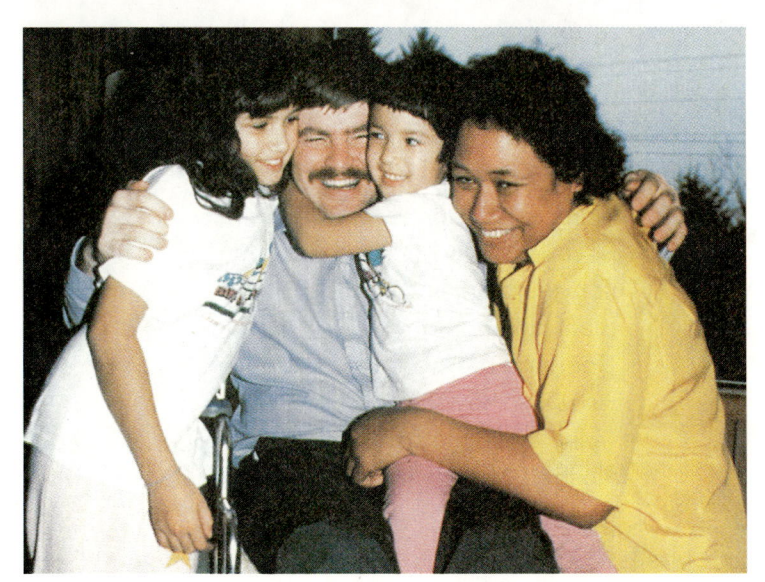

Peace Pledge

Find the missing words in the Dove of Peace. Write them on the lines.

(Dove contains words: help, joy, forgive, share)

I will _____ food with those who are hungry.

I will _____ those who hurt me.

I will bring _____ to those who are sad.

I will _____ those in need.

Jesus said, "My peace I give to you."
John 14:27

We Remember

What gifts do we offer God at the celebration of the Eucharist?
At the celebration of the Eucharist, with Jesus, we offer Jesus and ourselves to God.

Words to Know
Liturgy of the Eucharist

We Respond

May the Lord accept this sacrifice at your hands for the praise and glory of his name, for our good and the good of all his church.

from the Ordinary of the Mass

FAMILY CORNER

Jesus prays that all who gather in love as one family to share the meal of the Holy Eucharist will be one with him and with one another. That we may grow in this unity, he offers himself to the Father and comes to us in Holy Communion.

Read
John 6:51–58

Discuss
- Where did the Living Bread come from?
- What does Jesus promise to those who eat this Bread?
- When do we receive this Living Bread?
- How can we show Jesus that we appreciate his gift to us?

Pray
Lord, thank you for the bread to feed our bodies and the Eucharist to feed our souls.

- Think of an especially happy family meal. Recall the food, people present, conversation, and occasion. How did the meal help you grow closer as a family?
- Compare the meal with the eucharistic one. How are they alike? different?
- Make place mats for the family table. Illustrate them with wheat, grapes, a chalice, or other symbols of the Eucharist.
- Suggest ways to make mealtime happy.
- Make one Sunday of the month "Family Communion Sunday," when the family participates in Mass together.

❏ Signature

FAMILY FEATURE

A Family Prayer Corner

Today there is a renewed appreciation of the home as the domestic Church. The Catholic home is a place of prayer and the celebration of religious feasts. It is where life is infused with a spirit of unity and mutual support. One way to show that your family belongs to the Lord is to set up a prayer corner used as the focus of family prayer.

Because the Dershaws belong to the Byzantine Catholic Church, in their home they have an icon corner. It is in an east corner so that prayer is offered toward the rising sun, a symbol of Christ. An icon is a picture of Christ, Mary, or the saints that is venerated as a "window to heaven," a sacramental that makes present the holy ones depicted in it. Artists fast and pray when they paint icons.

The icons on the wall in the Dershaws' prayer corner include the patron saints of each family member. The icon of Theotokos (Mother of God) has been in the Dershaw family for generations. Above the icons is a cross. In front of them is a table with a Bible, other blessed items such as holy water and palm, and a tray of sand for holding tapers. A hanging lamp with a candle is kept burning. The candlelight makes the painting and gold leaf on the icons radiate. On the table there is also a censer with a handle. During prayer the Dershaws burn incense. On Saturday evening Mr. Dershaw carries it through the house in blessing to herald the start of the Lord's Day.

The Dershaws stand when they pray at their icon corner. They also gather there to observe significant moments in their lives. When Mr. Dershaw lost his job, he told the family the news at the icon corner. When Ann gets married, her parents will bless her there and present her with one of their icons for her new home. The Dershaws also have the custom of greeting the icon corner by bowing and making the Sign of the Cross or kissing the icons when they enter their home.

If you do not already have a prayer corner in your home, you may wish to arrange one using the religious items of your Catholic rite.

God's Many Gifts

Unscramble the letters in the gifts to name God's gifts. If you need help, look for the word on the page of the religion book given after the letters.

What can you give God for all God has given you?

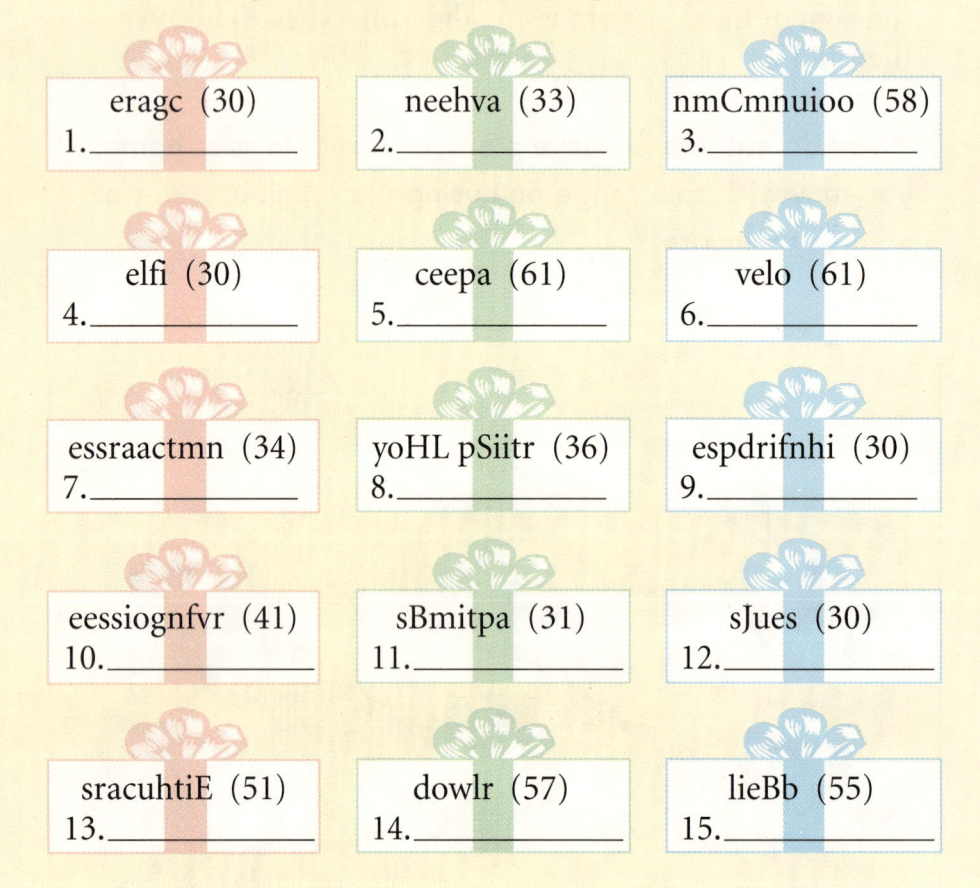

1. eragc (30) _____
2. neehva (33) _____
3. nmCmnuioo (58) _____
4. elfi (30) _____
5. ceepa (61) _____
6. velo (61) _____
7. essraactmn (34) _____
8. yoHL pSiitr (36) _____
9. espdrifnhi (30) _____
10. eessiognfvr (41) _____
11. sBmitpa (31) _____
12. sJues (30) _____
13. sracuhtiE (51) _____
14. dowlr (57) _____
15. lieBb (55) _____

(Answers: 1. grace, 2. heaven, 3. Communion, 4. life, 5. peace, 6. love, 7. sacraments, 8. Holy Spirit, 9. friendship, 10. forgiveness, 11. Baptism, 12. Jesus, 13. Eucharist, 14. world, 15. Bible)

God Is Great and Good

UNIT 3

God is revealed through his actions. In this unit the children come to know God through creation, his Word in Scripture, and his dealings with the chosen people. As they learn about God's promises, his saving acts in the exodus, his covenant of love, and through the gift of his commandments, they realize that God is great, good, faithful, powerful, loving, holy, merciful, and just. They are inspired to trust in God's promises to us and live out their baptismal covenant.

12 We Believe God Keeps Promises

Apostles' Creed

I believe in God, the Father almighty, creator of heaven and earth.
I believe in Jesus Christ, his only Son, our Lord.
He was conceived by the power of the Holy Spirit and born of the Virgin Mary.
He suffered under Pontius Pilate, was crucified, died, and was buried.
He descended to the dead.
On the third day he rose again.
He ascended into heaven and is seated at the right hand of the Father.
He will come again to judge the living and the dead.
I believe in the Holy Spirit, the holy catholic Church, the communion of saints, the forgiveness of sins, the resurrection of the body, and the life everlasting.
Amen.

We Profess Our Faith in the Creed

At each Sunday Eucharist the priest invites us to profess, or declare, our faith. We, the people of God, stand and pray the Creed.

A **creed** tells what we believe as Catholics. One form is the Apostles' Creed. By saying the Creed, we profess our belief in the great mysteries of our faith.

Mysteries of Our Faith

Complete the missing words to tell the main truths God has revealed.

1. God is the F ___ ___ ___ ___ ___ , who created all things.

2. God is the S ___ ___ , who redeemed us by his death and resurrection.

3. God is the Holy S ___ ___ ___ ___ ___ , who makes us holy.

4. The Catholic C ___ ___ ___ ___ ___ was founded by Jesus to teach us and make us holy.

We Can Grow in Faith

A newborn baby is small and weak. He or she needs good food, care, education, and love in order to grow. A child must also work hard to develop his or her powers. Our faith too should grow.

Pick a Puzzle Piece

Complete these sentences about ways we grow in faith. Use the words in the puzzle pieces.

1. We read God's Word in the _____.

2. We receive Jesus as our food in _____.

3. We listen when the _____ teaches us.

4. We tell what we believe as Christians, or _____ our faith.

5. We exercise our faith when we _____ God.

6. We speak to God and listen to God when we _____.

Studying your faith makes it grow. This book will help you learn what Catholics believe.

Puzzle pieces: profess, Holy Communion, sacrament, pray, obey, Church, Bible

65

God Our Creator Is Good

What kind of person would make the things shown here?

Write a word that describes the person who might make the thing in each picture.

We believe God made the universe and all of us. From the pictures, you see that our God is wonderful. Best of all, this great and wonderful God loves us.

We believe there is only one God. There are three Persons in God: Father, Son, and Holy Spirit. All three Persons are great, good, and loving. We praise and thank them in prayer.

Glory to God in the highest.
Luke 2:14

66

God Kept His Promises to the Israelites

To Abraham, the father of the chosen people, God had promised,

> "I will give this land of Canaan to your children."
> adapted from Genesis 12:7

After many years the children of Abraham, called Israelites, moved to Egypt. Pharaoh, the king of Egypt, became afraid of them. He thought they might become too powerful, so he made them slaves.

The Israelites were slaves in Egypt for many years. Then God chose Moses to lead them to freedom.

The story the Jewish people tell about their escape is in the Bible. In this story God spoke to Moses from a flaming bush. God said,

> "I have seen how my people suffer in Egypt. Now I have come to free them. I will bring them into a good land, the land of Canaan. You must lead my people out of Egypt. Tell Pharaoh what I have said."
> adapted from Exodus 3:7–10

Moses told Pharaoh God's message, but Pharaoh wouldn't let the Israelites go. Instead, he made them work even harder. Moses warned Pharaoh that terrible things would happen, but Pharaoh still refused to free his slaves.

God sent many signs of his power. Even then, Pharaoh wouldn't let God's people go. Finally, God told Moses to prepare his people for one more sign. Each family should kill a lamb and put its blood on the door of the house. God said,

> "It is the Passover of the LORD! This night every first-born son will die. But the blood will mark the houses where you are. Death will pass over you."
> adapted from Exodus 12:11–13

That night every oldest son died—even Pharaoh's son—but the Israelites were passed over. Then Pharaoh and all the Egyptians begged the Israelites to leave. God helped Moses lead his people across the Red Sea through the desert to Canaan. God is **faithful.** God keeps his promises.

68

God Keeps His Promise to Us

God promised to send us a Savior. God kept this promise. He sent his Son to save us from sin. His name, *Jesus*, means "God saves." Jesus' suffering, death, and resurrection freed us from sin. He won eternal life for us.

Now we are God's people on a journey to heaven. Jesus shows us the way through his Holy Spirit. He helps us meet temptations. Jesus has a place ready for us.

Our journey is like the Israelites'. As God kept his promise to them, he will keep his to us. God will lead us to eternal life if we trust in his promise and do what he tells us.

Word Wheel

Fill in the missing words. Start with *I* at the top of the Word Wheel. Print it, and then every second letter, on a blank. Continue until you can read Jesus' promises.

___ am the resurrection and the life;

whoever ___ ___ ___ ___ ___ ___ ___ ___

in me, even if he dies, will ___ ___ ___ ___ .
                              John 11:25

Whoever ___ ___ ___ ___ my flesh and

___ ___ ___ ___ ___ ___ my blood has

eternal ___ ___ ___ ___ , and I shall raise

him on the ___ ___ ___ ___ day.
                       John 6:54

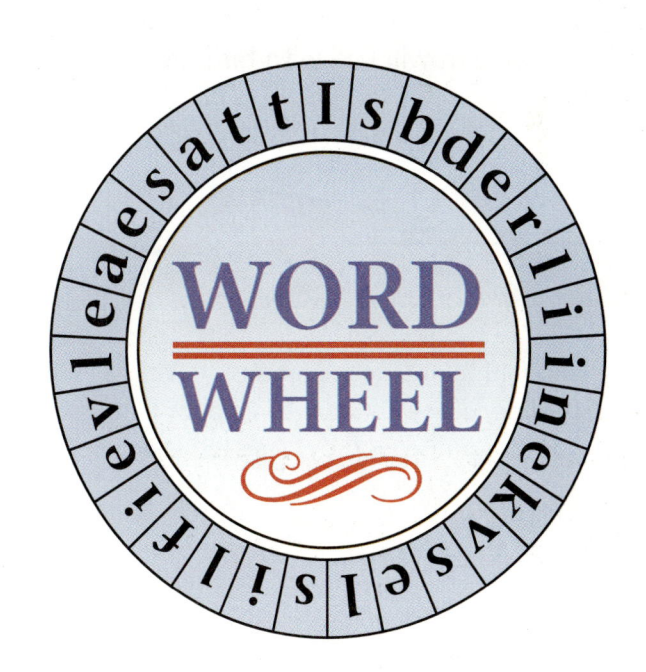

Checking Your Understanding

Put the words in order to form sentences about God. Write the sentences on the lines.

1. _____.
   created   One   everything   God   almighty

2. _____.
   Persons   God   three   There   are   in   one

3. _____.
   promises   keeps   God   his   all

4. _____.
   God   us   trust   wants   to   him   obey   and

We Remember

Where are the chief truths of our faith found?
The chief truths of our faith are in the Creed.

What does God promise us?
God promises that those who believe in him and obey him will live with him eternally in heaven.

Words to Know
profess   creed

Words to Memorize
Apostles' Creed

We Respond

Jesus, I hope in you.

FAMILY CORNER

God's actions show his greatness, goodness, and faithfulness to his promises. With confidence we can turn to God for help each day. We praise God by living as his children.

Read
John 11:25–27

Discuss
- What do you think is the greatest thing God has done? the most wonderful thing God has made?
- What does Jesus ask us to do?
- What does Jesus promise us?
- How can we grow in faith as a family?

Pray
O how good is the good God!

Do
- Take a nature walk or visit a natural history museum. Share how things you see speak of God's greatness.
- Share how God has helped you. Then form a circle, hold hands, and thank God.
- After a meal discuss God's gifts to you that day. Take turns praying grace and thanking God for particular gifts.

_____
❑ Signature

13 God Is Powerful and Loving

God Saves the Israelites with His Power
Pharaoh was sorry that he had let the Israelites go. He sent his army to bring them back.

The Israelites were afraid when they saw Pharaoh's army. "Do not be afraid," Moses told them. "The Lord will win a great victory for you today." God said to Moses, "Stretch out your hand over the sea and split it so that the people may pass through it."

Moses did what God told him. All night God sent a strong wind. He made a path of dry land. The Israelites marched into the sea with water like walls on both sides of them.

All Pharaoh's horses and soldiers went into the sea after the Israelites. God said to Moses, "Stretch out your hand over the sea again." Moses did, and the sea flowed back upon Pharaoh's army.

The Israelites rejoiced. Their **all-powerful** God had saved them.

based on Exodus 14:10–28

Moses and the men sang a song of victory and praise to God while the women danced.

> **Moses' Song of Victory**
>
> I will sing to the Lord for he has won a great victory!
>
> The horses and their riders he has cast into the sea.
>
> The Lord gives me strength and courage, and he has been my Savior.
>
> Who is like you, O Lord? Who is like you, worker of wonders?
>
> In your mercy you led the people you saved; in your strength you guided them to their own land.
>
> adapted from Exodus 15:1–2, 11, 13

We also trust in God's power. It is almighty God who frees us from our greatest enemy, sin. God helps us win battles against it. He brings us safely to our heavenly home.

A Pyramid Puzzle

Fill in the missing words. You can find them on the pyramid.

God is all-_____ .

God helps those who _____ and _____ him.

I will ask God to _____ me.

I will _____ in God's power.

help
powerful
trust
obey

72

God Fed the Israelites

The Israelites had to wander through the desert. They felt tired, hungry, and thirsty. God said, "I will rain down bread from heaven."

The next morning something that looked like frost covered the ground. "What is this?" the Israelites asked.

Moses told them, "This is the bread the Lord has given you to eat."

Each morning this white bread covered the ground. The Israelites called it **manna.** The Lord told them, "Take only what you need for one day." He wanted his people to trust in his care. They showed their trust by doing what God told them.

God fed his people manna until they came to Canaan. He looked after them like a **loving father** and a caring mother.

based on Exodus 16:1–35

Psalm Prayer

Give thanks to the LORD for he is good,
  for his love is everlasting.
Who alone does great wonders,
  for his love is everlasting.
Who led his people through the wilderness,
  for his love is everlasting.
Give thanks to the God of heaven,
  for his love is everlasting.

adapted from Psalm 136:1, 4, 16, 26

God Feeds Us

God shows loving care for us today. He feeds us with the Body and Blood of his own Son, Jesus, in the Holy Eucharist. Jesus is the bread from heaven. Once he said,

> "I am the living bread that came down from heaven; whoever eats this bread will live forever; and the bread that I will give is my flesh, for the life of the world."
>
> John 6:51

This heavenly food nourishes the life we received in Baptism. It strengthens us on our journey through this world to the promised land of heaven.

In Holy Communion we are united with Jesus. He shares himself with us in love. He makes us more like himself. He also comes to make us more united as his people. Talk to Jesus as your friend when you receive him in Holy Communion. The word *a-l-t-a-r* will help you remember five things to do in your prayer.

Adore God. Tell God how great and good he is.
Love God. Tell God how much you love him.
Thank God for something special.
Ask God to help you, your family, and all people.
Resolve to do something special to show God your love.

Write a prayer to say after Holy Communion.

_____

_____

_____

_____

God Makes a Covenant of Love

God and the Israelites made a **covenant** of love with each other. The Bible tells us about this important agreement.

The Israelites came to Mt. Sinai in the desert and pitched camp. Then Moses went up the mountain to God. God gave him this message for the people:

> "You have seen how I saved you. If you listen to my words, you shall be dearer to me than all other people. You will be a holy nation."

On the third day God gave the people the **commandments.** They answered,

"Everything the Lord has said, we will do."

Later God gave Moses the law written on stone tablets. The people loved God's law. They knew it would guide them to happiness. It showed God's love for them.

The Israelites were bound to God as his own people. He was their God, and they belonged to him. They would obey his laws. God would bless them and care for them. God and his people were united in a covenant of love.

based on Exodus 19:1–20:17; 24:1–12

We Have a Covenant with God

We are the people of God today. We too are bound to God in a covenant of love. Through Baptism God has made us his own children. We have received a share in his life. We have promised to live by his laws and follow Jesus. God has promised that we will live with him forever in heaven.

How may these children be keeping their covenant of love?

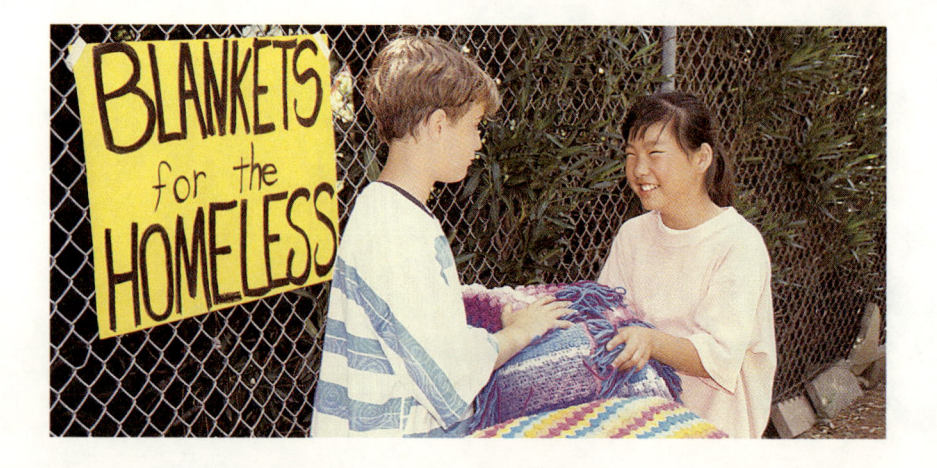

An Acrostic on *Covenant*
Write the words where they belong in the puzzle.

1. God ____ us to be his children.
2. God showed his ____ in saving his people.
3. God gave us his laws of ____ .
4. We are God's ____ today.
5. God makes us his ____ people.
6. The commandments are God's ____ .
7. God made a ____ with his people.
8. We became God's children at our ____ .

We Remember

What is our covenant of love with God?
Our covenant of love is our agreement with God. God makes us his children, and we obey his laws and follow Jesus.

Words to Know

covenant   commandment

We Respond

I will celebrate your favors forever, LORD.
I will always proclaim your love.
   adapted from Psalm 89:2

FAMILY CORNER

Almighty God works wonders for those who love him. How we should value our covenant of love with the Lord and desire to obey him!

Read
Exodus 19:4

Discuss
- Why did God punish the Egyptians?
- What did God mean when he spoke of carrying the Israelites "on eagles' wings"?
- How does God carry us on eagles' wings?
- How can we show our gratitude to God?

Pray
You are mighty, Lord!

Do
- Discuss the importance of agreements in everyday living (in business, marriage contracts, purchases, school assignments, helping neighbors).
- Make a written agreement or covenant with a family member to exchange services or favors this coming week. Each evening check on how everyone has kept his or her part of the bargain.
- Share with the family some experience you have had or read about that showed God's mighty power or his tender love. Thank him by singing a song of praise, such as "Holy God" or "Mighty Lord."

_____
❑ Signature

77

14 God Is Holy and Great

The Lord Our God Is Holy

Have you ever felt God's holy presence in a special way? It fills us with wonder and awe.

How did God first speak to Moses? God said from the burning bush: "Come no nearer! Remove the sandals from your feet, for the place where you stand is holy ground. I am the God of your fathers." Moses hid his face, for he was afraid.

adapted from Exodus 3:5–6

Before the **all-holy** God we feel, like Moses, small and helpless. We fear God, and it is right that we should. But our fear of God is full of *love* and *praise*. We know that the great and holy God loves us.

God revealed his holiness through his Son, Jesus. Jesus is the holy One of God.

- Jesus performed miracles.
- Jesus did works of holiness.
- Jesus rose from the dead.

Write two things Jesus did because he is holy.

1. _____

2. _____

How do we show that we are holy people?

God revealed his holy name to Moses. Moses said to the Lord, "When the Israelites ask your name, what am I to tell them?"

The Lord answered, "I am who am."

"I AM WHO AM"

adapted from Exodus 3:13–14

Names were very important to the Israelites. A person's name told not only who he or she was. It revealed something about the person. God's name tells who he is. He is God, the holy One. God's name means God himself.

We worship God with love and praise because he is the holy One. The second commandment tells us to speak God's name with love and reverence. It tells us to respect everything related to God.

Can You Find Signs of the Holy?
Unscramble the words to find persons and things used in the service of God.
(*Clue:* Look at the picture.)

1. streip _____

2. taral _____

3. celaich _____

4. cixfuric _____

5. Bleib _____

6. mnostarcne _____

79

A Special Dwelling

The **great** God was with his chosen people. He told Moses, "My people must build me a special dwelling. I wish to dwell among them."

When the dwelling was complete, God gave a special sign of his presence. A bright cloud came to rest over it.

It was by this cloud that God led his people on their journey. When the cloud rose, the Israelites took down their tents and the dwelling. They followed the cloud until it stopped. Then they pitched their tents and put the dwelling in the center of the camp.

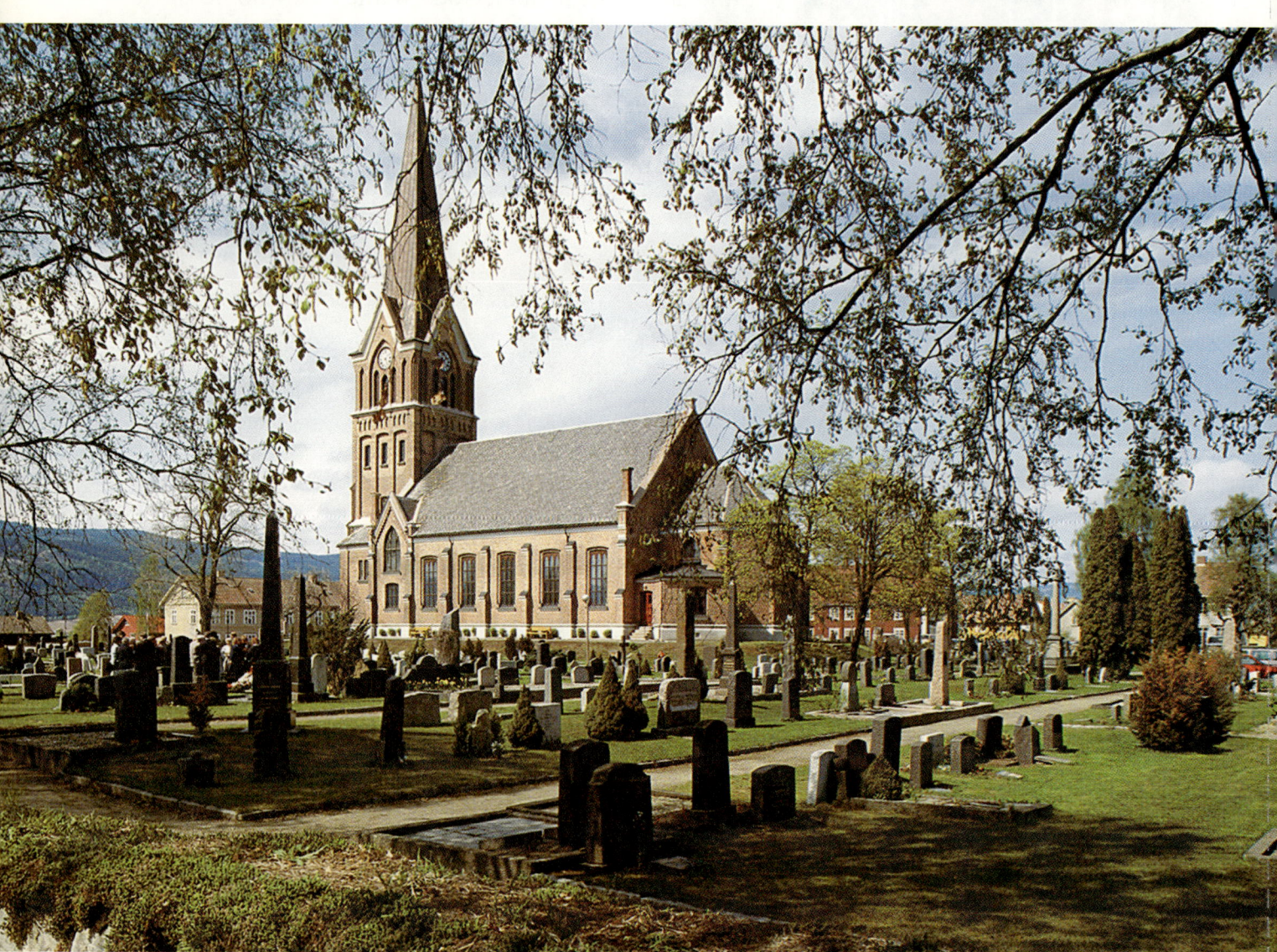

Jesus Dwells among Us

Later, God came to dwell among his people in an even more wonderful way.

God's own Son came to earth as man. Jesus was God living among his people. He shared their work, play, joys, and sorrows. God was still caring for his people.

Jesus still dwells among his people. He is with us in his Church through the Holy Spirit. He dwells in our hearts by grace. The same Jesus who was with his people in Israel is present in the Blessed Sacrament in our churches. He is with us, guiding us and caring for us with his power and his love.

God Is Everywhere

God is so great! Besides being in special places, God is also everywhere. This is wonderful because God is with every one of the people he has created and loves.

God Knows All Things about His People

God knows all things. He knows everything about each person. God knows what we think and how we feel. He knows even the secrets of our hearts. He knows when we are in need of help even when we don't tell anyone. God is with us and wants to help us.

God Knows All about the Universe

God, who created the universe, knows all about it. He knows how mountains came to be and how seeds grow. He knows the center of the earth and the most-distant star.

God knows everything that is happening now. He knows about things that happened long ago. He knows all that will happen in the future. And God uses everything for our good.

**Praise to you, O holy God!
You are present everywhere.
You know all things.
You are so great.**

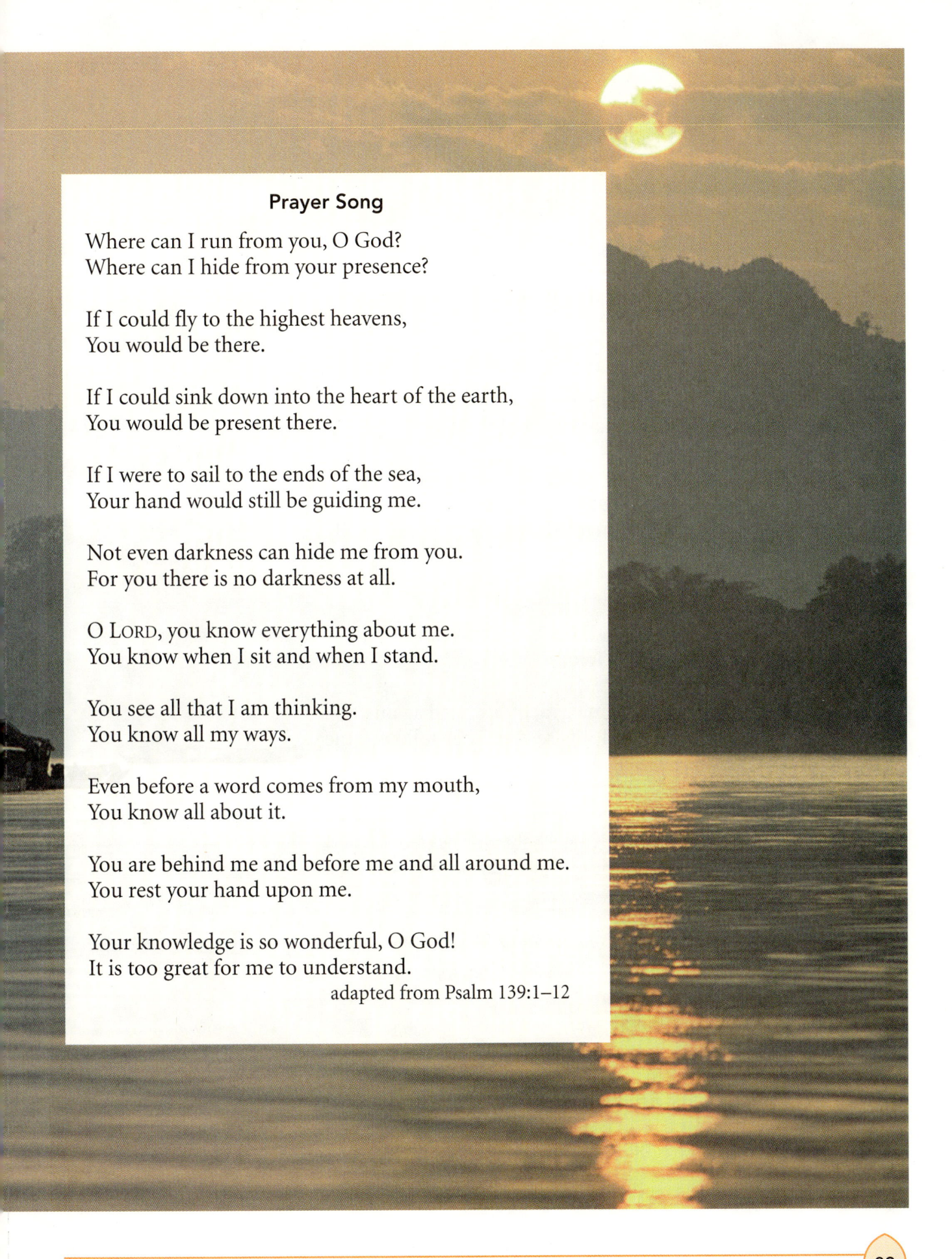

Prayer Song

Where can I run from you, O God?
Where can I hide from your presence?

If I could fly to the highest heavens,
You would be there.

If I could sink down into the heart of the earth,
You would be present there.

If I were to sail to the ends of the sea,
Your hand would still be guiding me.

Not even darkness can hide me from you.
For you there is no darkness at all.

O LORD, you know everything about me.
You know when I sit and when I stand.

You see all that I am thinking.
You know all my ways.

Even before a word comes from my mouth,
You know all about it.

You are behind me and before me and all around me.
You rest your hand upon me.

Your knowledge is so wonderful, O God!
It is too great for me to understand.

adapted from Psalm 139:1–12

Elijah and the Prophets of Baal: A Play

God—*the one, true God*—is worthy to have first place in our lives.

Act One

Reader 1: Moses spoke to the people of Israel in the desert. He told them the first great commandment of the Lord.

Moses: Hear, O Israel! The Lord is our God, the Lord alone! Therefore, you shall love the Lord your God, with all your heart and soul and with all your strength. Take to heart these words which I command you today!

People: We will!

Act Two

Reader 2: Many years passed. Some Israelites sinned against the true God. They worshiped Baal, a false god. They followed the sinful ways of their pagan neighbors.

Reader 3: God sent the prophet Elijah to call his people back to worship him alone. Elijah met King Ahab and the people of Israel on Mt. Carmel. Four hundred and fifty prophets of Baal were there too.

Elijah: Listen to me! How long will you try to be on two sides at once? If the Lord is God, follow him! But if Baal is God, follow Baal.

Reader 4: The people did not answer.

Elijah: Bring me two bulls. We will offer one to Baal and the other to the God of Israel. Place them on the altar but do not start a fire. You will call on Baal. I will call on the Lord. The God who answers by burning the bull on the altar is the true God.

People: Let it be so!

Reader 3: The prophets of Baal placed a bull on the altar. From morning until noon they called to their god.

Prophets of Baal: O Baal, answer us! Send fire.

Reader 4: But there was no answer. So the priests of Baal danced around the altar. Still no fire came.

Elijah: Call louder! Perhaps your god is sleeping or has gone on a journey!

Prophets of Baal: O Baal, answer us!

Reader 1: Still there was no answer. Then Elijah called the people to come near him. He built an altar of stones and set wood on it. He dug a deep trench around the altar. Elijah laid the second bull on the altar. He ordered the men to pour water over the bull and the wood.

Reader 2: Three times water was poured over the bull, flowed down the altar, and filled the trench. Elijah prayed.

Elijah: Lord God of Abraham, let everyone know that you are God of Israel and I am your servant. Answer me.

Reader 4: At once the fire of the Lord came down. It burned the bull, the altar, the stones, and even the water in the trench. The people fell with their faces to the ground.

People: The Lord is God! The Lord is God!

based on Deuteronomy 6:4–6 and 1 Kings 18:16–39

Dedicated Christian lay leaders today give God first place in their lives.

Benedict Kiwanuka was put to death when he refused to sign unjust death sentences. He is known as the Thomas More of Africa.

Thomas More was a great lawyer long ago in England. Because he obeyed God instead of the king, he was beheaded.

How Well Do You Remember?

Complete these sentences with the correct words. One letter belongs in each box.

1. God is ☐ ☐ ☐ y.

2. God is present
☐ v ☐ ☐ y ☐ ☐ e ☐ ☐.

3. God knows ☐ l ☐ things.

4. God is ☐ ☐ w ☐ ☐ ☐ with us.

5. God knows even the secrets of our ☐ ☐ a ☐ ☐ ☐.

6. God is present in a special way in ☐ h ☐ r ☐ ☐.

We Remember

What is God like?
God is holy and great. He is everywhere and always near. He knows all things.

How does the second commandment tell us to show reverence for God?
The second commandment tells us to show reverence for God by honoring his holy name. It tells us to respect everything related to God.

We Respond

Praise the Lord: the Lord is good!
Sing to God's name; it is gracious.

Psalm 135:3

FAMILY CORNER

The holiness and greatness of God are beyond our understanding. Incredibly, this holy and great God is with us and guides us with his love.

Read
Exodus 4:10–17

Discuss
- Why did Moses say he could not go to Pharaoh?
- How did God promise to help him?
- How is God with us as he was with Moses?
- How does God help us to know what to say?

Pray
Stay with me, Lord!

Do
- Compose a litany, like the following, to praise and thank God for his loving care:
  All respond, "We praise and thank you, O Lord."
  Father, you are all holy . . .
  For calling us to be holy . . .
- Make a family visit to the Blessed Sacrament in your parish church. While you are there, pray your litany.
- Invite the family to a bubble-blowing party. This can be a time of awareness that God is present and wants you to be happy. Unlike bubbles, God's love, as well as the happiness he gives, lasts.

❏ Signature

15 God Is Just and Merciful

Lord God, have mercy on your people.

Our Just and Merciful God Loves Us

At times God's chosen people kept his commandments. God blessed them with peace and happiness. At other times the Israelites did not keep their covenant. Their sins brought trouble. Their rulers became selfish and foolish. The people were no longer united, and the nation became weak. Enemies attacked. In order to bring the people back to him, God allowed these sufferings. From this we learn that God is **just**.

But at the same time God is very **merciful**. He knew that his people were weak and sinful. He was always ready to forgive them and take them back.

Moses often spoke to God for his people. He prayed, "Lord, have mercy on your people. Do not look upon their sins."

The people cried to God for mercy too. God always had pity on them. He forgave them again and again.

Psalm Prayer

Bless the LORD, O my soul,
    and remember all his kindness.
The LORD is merciful and kind,
    slow to anger and most loving.
God does not punish us
    as our sins and wrongs deserve.
Just as the heavens are high
    above the earth
    so great is his kindness toward
    those who fear him.
God puts our sins farther away
    than the east is from the west.
As a father has pity on his
    children,
    so the LORD has pity
    on those who fear him.
    adapted from Psalm 103:2, 8–13

God shows us justice and mercy, too. When we sin, he allows suffering to bring us back to him. When we keep his laws of love, he blesses us with peace. He forgives our sins when we are sorry. As the Good Shepherd, he welcomes us back and cares for us.

Use the code below and complete the sentence.

We believe that our God is

___ ___ ___ ___ ___ ___ ___ ___
 7   2   9   1   4   3   8   6

and ___ ___ ___ ___ .
        5   8   10   11

C	E	F	I	J	L	M	U	R	S	T
1	2	3	4	5	6	7	8	9	10	11

Jesus Revealed the Father's Justice and Mercy

Jesus revealed the justice and mercy of God our Father. He showed justice when he drove out the people selling things in the Temple. He showed mercy when he healed the sick and forgave sinners.

To show that God is *just*, Jesus told a story about a rich man and a poor man. The rich man had fine clothes and plenty of good food. The poor man, called Lazarus, longed to have the leftovers from the rich man's table. The rich man would not give him any. Then one day Lazarus died and went to a place of happiness. When the rich man died, he went to a place of suffering. In this story we see that evil deeds are punished and good ones rewarded.

Jesus tells us of God's *mercy* in many stories. Write the name of one here.

_____

_____

Jesus wanted to teach us that God our Father is merciful when we are sorry for our sins. He forgives us and invites us to celebrate his goodness.

Jesus wants us to be just and merciful as he is. We are just when we treat others as we would like to be treated. We are merciful when we forgive others as our heavenly Father forgives us. We show his merciful love when we help those in need.

A Challenge for You!
Complete this puzzle on our just and merciful God. Use the clues.

1. We pray for mercy at the beginning of _____ .
2. When we forgive others, we show _____ .
3. When the Israelites were sorry they sinned, God _____ them.
4. When we obey God's commandments, God gives us _____ .
5. God has _____ on us who are weak.
6. _____ can bring us back to God.
7. We are _____ when we treat each other fairly.
8. Jesus told us to _____ one another.

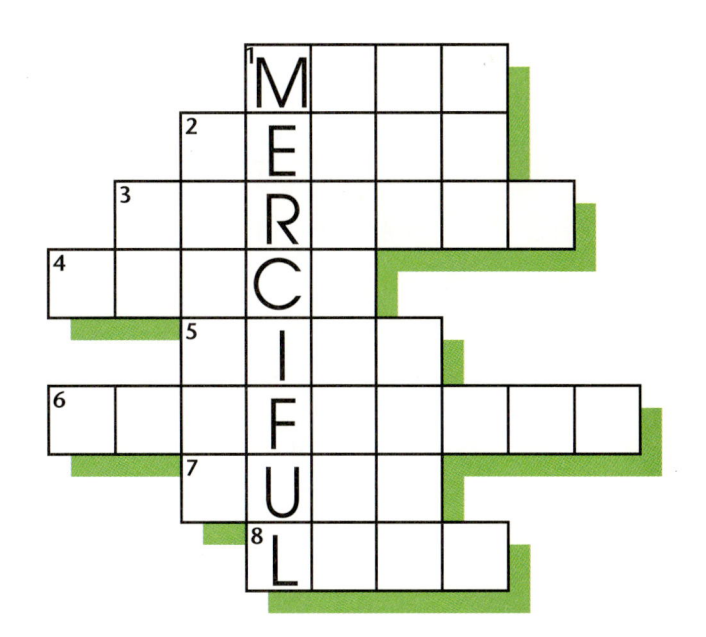

89

God is love. 1 John 4:8

What Is God Like?

In the box are some of the wonderful truths about God.

Write, below the verses from the Bible, what each passage tells us about God. Use a phrase from the box to complete each truth.

> **GOD**
> keeps his promises
> is almighty
> is just and merciful
> cares for his people
> knows all things

1. "I will save you with my mighty acts." (adapted from Exodus 6:6)

   God _____.

2. "I will give you the land of Canaan as I promised your father, Abraham." (adapted from Exodus 6:8)

   God _____.

3. "Pharaoh . . . would not listen . . . just as the LORD had foretold." (Exodus 7:13)

   God _____.

4. "This is the bread which the LORD has given you to eat." (Exodus 16:15)

   God _____.

5. "The LORD is a merciful God, slow to anger and rich in kindness, forgiving sin." (adapted from Exodus 34:6–7)

   God _____.

Make a Journey

> **Fill in** the blanks with the words in the sun.
> **Find** your score. Circle the place you reached.
>
> 10 Promised Land
> 8 or 9 Mt. Sinai
> 6 or 7 Desert
> 4 or 5 Red Sea

Baptism Eucharist
caring Holy One
covenant merciful
everywhere power
faithful
forgiveness

1. God freed the Israelites from slavery and showed his great _____ .

2. God and the people of Israel were united in a holy _____ .

3. We are united to God in a covenant by our _____ .

4. God always keeps his promises, so we say that he is _____ .

5. Jesus feeds us in a special way in the _____ .

6. God is always ready to forgive our sins. He is _____ .

7. God fed his people in the desert. He is loving and _____ .

8. We worship God because he is the _____ .

9. In the Sacrament of the Reconciliation we receive God's _____ .

10. God is present _____ .

Word Search

Circle twelve words in the puzzle that describe God. Then write the three words that you like best.

_____

_____

_____

```
T R E M F P O W E R F U L
A G R E A T R U T H F U L
M E R C I F U L L A P I M
L J U S T G D T O R P E C
R O S W H O L Y V T V W I
U T M I F O R G I V I N G
S B D S U D Z P N R E T O
C O R E L J M I G H T Y N
```

We Remember

How is God just?
God allows us to suffer for our sins, and he rewards us for the good we do.

How is God merciful?
God shows us his mercy by forgiving our sins when we are sorry.

We Respond

I will treat others as they should be treated and as I would like to be treated. I will forgive others as my heavenly Father forgives me and will help those in need.

FAMILY CORNER

God is just and merciful to everyone. Let us appreciate God's goodness to us and realize that to be holy as God is, we must be just and merciful to others.

Read
Psalm 103:8–10, 17–18

Discuss
- How does the psalmist tell about God's justice?
- How is God's mercy explained?
- How can we show justice and mercy as our heavenly Father does?

Pray
O God, be merciful to me, a sinner!

Do
- Family members can easily hurt one another by thoughtless words or actions. Discuss ways of asking forgiveness and ways of showing forgiveness. Resolve to be particularly kind to a specific member of the family.
- As a family, watch a television program—preferably a drama or one about a family situation. Discuss how the characters show, or fail to show, justice or mercy.
- Choose phrases from the Our Father. These may be written on slips of paper or spoken. Share the meaning of the phrases, especially as they refer to justice or mercy. Conclude by joining hands in a circle and praying or singing the Our Father.

_____
❑ Signature

We Celebrate the Greatness and Goodness of God

Leader: We have come to worship the Lord together. Let us sing to God with joy!

Song   **We Gather Together**

We gather together to sing the Lord's praises,
To worship the Father through Jesus his Son.
In this celebration all sing with jubilation.
We are God's holy people whose freedom he won.

Our Lord and Creator, our Father, we praise you!
Your greatness and goodness to us you have shown.
You, Lord, are beside us. In love you lead and guide us.
You have redeemed and called us and made us your own.

Leader: Long ago God revealed his greatness and goodness in the wonderful things he did. He freed the Israelites from slavery and saved them from their enemies. He invited them to be his people and to let him guide them.

Reader: Give thanks to the Lord, call his name,
proclaim his deeds to the people!
Sing to him, sing his praises,
tell about all his wondrous deeds!
Glory in his holy name.
Rejoice, O hearts, that seek the Lord!
       adapted from Psalm 105:1–3

Psalm Prayer

Group 1: Sing joyfully to the Lord, all you lands.
Serve the Lord with gladness.
Come before him with joyful song.

Group 2: Know that the Lord is God. He made us.
We belong to him. We are his people, the sheep he tends.

Group 1: Give thanks to the Lord. Praise his holy name.
The Lord Yahweh is good.

Group 2: His kindness and his faithfulness never end.
adapted from Psalm 100

Song

Leader: God cares for us with great love. He sent his Son to save us. Jesus stays with us. He feeds us with his own Body and Blood. Let us praise and thank God for his goodness to us.

Group 1: You care for all your children with love.
We give you thanks and praise!

Group 2: You feed us with the Bread of life.
We thank you for this Living Bread!

Group 1: You dwell among us in your holy Church.
We want to stay close to you.

Group 2: You are faithful and true to your promises.
We trust you. We believe all you have said.

Group 1: You love us with an endless love.
We want to love you more, O Lord our God!

Group 2: You are so great and so good!
We thank you for yourself!

Leader: O God our Father, we have praised you in song and prayer. We also want to live out our worship by serving you in all our brothers and sisters. Help us to do this always. Amen.

Silent Prayer

Think of a special way in which you will try to serve God better today. Tell God about it. Ask him to help you.

All: Our Father . . .

FAMILY FEATURE

Epiphany: Jesus Is Made Known to the Gentiles

Tina Diaz lives in Puerto Rico. She looks forward to Epiphany, or Three Kings' Day, when her family celebrates the manifestation of Jesus to the Gentiles. Long ago the Lord's birthday was celebrated on January 6. By A.D. 400, however, Christmas was celebrated on December 25, and January 6 commemorated the visit of the Magi, or three kings.

On the night before Epiphany, Tina puts straw or grass in her shoes or in a box for the kings' camels. She sets this on the windowsill or under her bed, along with a bowl of water. In the morning she finds presents there. During the day the family visits relatives where the kings have left more gifts for the children. The Diaz family always does something for the poor that day. Sometimes they give a party to which each guest brings a gift for the poor.

In Italy the gift bringer on Epiphany is Befana, an old woman. According to a legend, Befana was invited by the Magi to accompany them to the newborn king. But Befana delayed in order to clean her home and finish her baking. As a result she missed seeing the Christ Child. Befana atones for her negligence by giving gifts to good children in her travels through the world.

Epiphany is celebrated in Europe with a Three Kings' Cake. Inside the cake, which is like a large cookie, there is a dried bean, a thimble, a dime, or another treasure. Whoever finds the object in his or her piece of cake supposedly will have wealth in the coming year or become king or queen of an Epiphany party.

You might transfer some of your celebration of Christmas to the Epiphany, which in the United States is on the Sunday between January 2 and 8. Then December 25 may be kept as a more spiritual feast.

Three Kings' Cake (serves 12)

1/2 cup blanched almonds
1 cup sugar
6 tablespoons soft butter
1 teaspoon vanilla or almond extract
2 eggs lightly beaten
2 1/4 cups flour
1 1/2 teaspoons baking powder
2 tablespoons raisins or currants
fortune, such as a bean or a dime

Grind the almonds with 1/4 cup sugar in a food processor or blender. In a bowl blend the butter and remaining sugar with a fork. Then beat in the extract and the eggs, saving a tablespoon of beaten egg for glaze. Place the flour and baking powder in a sieve and sift it into the mixture, stirring constantly. Stir in the almond-sugar mix, raisins or currants, and fortune. Put the dough on a greased cookie sheet and flatten it into a circle 1/2 inch thick. Brush the remainder of the egg over the cake. Bake at 350° F for 20 minutes.

What's God Like?

Match each story with what it shows about God.
A. God is merciful.
B. God is everywhere.
C. God knows everything.

_____ A little boy was afraid to get a broom out of a dark closet. Remembering what his mother told him about God, he called out, "God, if you're in there, would you hand me the broom?"

_____ Dennis the Menace kneels at his bed and prays, "I'm sorry, but I'm afraid I had a real interesting day again today."

_____ A mother said, "Look at that. The sun and moon are both out at the same time." Her little girl responded, "Don't worry, Mom. God knows what he's doing."

(Answers: B, A, C)

Comparing

Check the words from Israel's story that are part of our lives.

_____ covenant   _____ God's saving power
_____ Baal   _____ Pharaoh
_____ Commandments   _____ bread from heaven
_____ God's dwelling   _____ slavery

The Greatest

Color the areas that have a dot to find out who is the most wonderful one of all.

God's Goodness

In the box draw or write about something that shows how good God is to you.

(Answers: all checked but Baal, Pharaoh, and slavery)

God's Plan Is a Plan of Love

UNIT 4

God's great love is manifested in Jesus, our Redeemer, who made eternal life possible for us. In this unit the children learn about the events surrounding the coming of Jesus. With Simeon they recognize Jesus as the Messiah, who brought God's kingdom to earth. Jesus' baptism and his temptations mark the beginning of his public mission. His miracles show that the kingdom has come, and his parables teach us about that kingdom. The children are encouraged to belong to God's kingdom of love by keeping God's laws and following the example of Jesus.

16 God Created People to Share His Life

We Have Natural Powers

Here is Buttons enjoying a book of poems. You can see that a plan for a new doghouse is passing through his mind.

Silly? Make-believe? Of course! Animals can't really read or make plans. They have an animal nature, not a human nature. It is not natural for an animal to think or read a book. Human beings have greater powers than animals. Human beings can **think**, **choose**, and **love.**

Suppose we could give Buttons the human powers of thinking, choosing, and loving. He would still be a dog—but a dog with human powers. He would have **supernatural** powers for a dog. *Super-* means "above" or "greater." What do you think *supernatural* means?

Scripture says that God created human beings in his own image and likeness, male and female. God made them equal. They are to work as partners to care for God's world and everyone in it.

Adam and Eve Shared in God's Life

God gave the first man and woman an even greater gift than human life. God gave them a share in his own life. It was a supernatural life, which made them God's own children so that they could enjoy his friendship. Adam and Eve could never do anything to deserve this. God gave them this gift freely, out of love. That is why we call our sharing in God's life **grace.** *Grace* means "favor" or "gift."

Grace gives human beings the supernatural powers of **faith, hope,** and **love** of God. With these powers we can believe in God, hope in his promises, and love him. We can see and enjoy God forever in heaven.

```
C H O O S E
K G T R A N
N O H O P E
G R A C E W
I T P H R O
F H B E N H
T I E R A U
D N L P T M
S K I O U A
C N E W R N
L O V E A L
B R E R L W
```

Word Search

Write the missing words to finish the sentences below. Circle the answers in the puzzle.

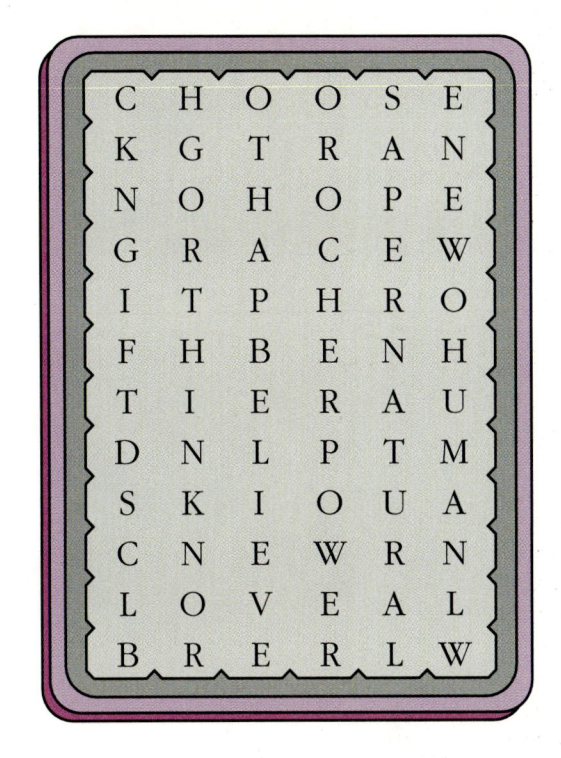

1. We have natural powers to _____ , _____ , and _____ .

2. Our share in God's life is called _____ .

3. *Grace* means "favor" or " _____ ."

4. Supernatural powers are above our _____ powers.

5. We have the supernatural powers to _____ in God, to _____ in God's promises, and to _____ God above all.

Sin Spoiled God's Plan for Us

A story in the Bible tells us that the devil wanted to destroy Adam and Eve's friendship with God. He tempted Adam and Eve to disobey God's law. The devil made what God had forbidden seem good. Eve freely chose to turn against God. She listened to the devil and ate forbidden fruit. Then she gave some to Adam, and he too chose to disobey God by eating. As soon as they had eaten the fruit, Adam and Eve felt ashamed.

Adam and Eve had turned from God's friendship. They lost the special gifts that had made them so happy. Their sin brought evil into the world. Evil would make them suffer. One day they would die.

This first sin spoiled God's plan of love. Now we are born in **original sin.** We have to struggle against evil. We sometimes desire to do sinful things. It is hard for us to choose what is truly good.

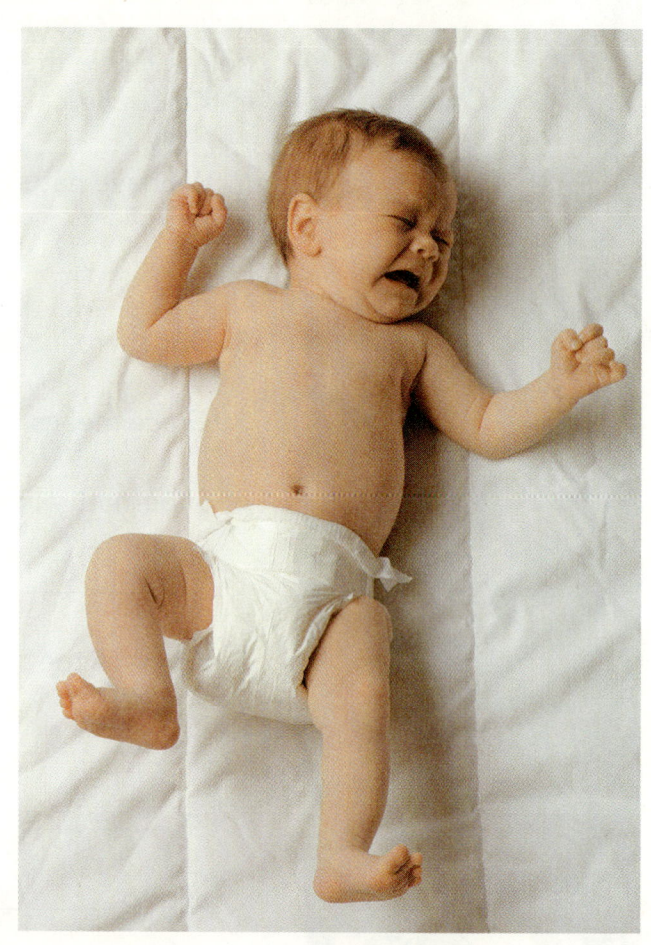

Jesus Is Our Redeemer

God still loved Adam and Eve. He promised a Redeemer to save all people from the power of sin and death. The Redeemer that God promised was his own Son, Jesus Christ. Through Jesus we can have the life of grace.

All that Jesus did pleased God his Father. All that Jesus taught shows us the way to happiness here and forever in heaven.

Jesus is present with us. He gives us all we need to be united with God. He offers himself to his heavenly Father for our sins.

Jesus helps us grow in love for God our Father and others. He helps us to be unselfish. He helps us forgive those who have hurt us. If we follow Jesus, we live in grace. We are freed from the power of sin.

Psalm Prayer

O Lord, our Lord,
how great is your name
over all the earth!

What is man that you should think of him,
or the son of man that you should care for him?

You have made him little less than the angels,
and crowned him with glory and honor.

O Lord, our Lord,
how great is your name over all the earth!
adapted from Psalm 8

The Story of Creation and the Fall: A Play

Reader 1: The LORD God formed man out of the clay of the earth and breathed life into him. Man became a living person.

Reader 2: In Eden the LORD God planted a garden with many kinds of beautiful trees. God put man into the garden to care for it and ordered:

God: You may eat from any tree except the tree in the middle of the garden. From that tree you must not eat. If you eat from it, you will surely die.

Reader 3: Then God said:

God: It is not good for man to be alone. I will make him a partner.

Reader 4: So from the ground God formed all the wild animals and the birds. God brought them to the man to name them. The man gave names to all the cattle, birds, and wild animals.

Reader 5: None was a good partner for the man. So God made the man fall into a deep sleep. While he slept, God took one of the man's ribs and formed a woman. God brought her to the man. The man said:

Adam: This at last is bone of my bone and flesh of my flesh. This is to be called "woman."

Reader 6: This is why a man leaves his father and mother and joins himself to his wife.

Reader 7: Now the serpent was the most cunning of all the animals. The serpent asked the woman:

Serpent: Did God really tell you not to eat from any of the trees in the garden?

Eve: We may eat the fruit of the trees except one. If we eat from that tree, we will die.

Serpent: You certainly will not die! God knows that when you eat of it, you will be like God. You will know good and evil.

Reader 8: Now the woman thought of how good it would be to eat the fruit and become like God, so she took some of the fruit and ate it. Then she gave some to the man and he also ate. As soon as they had eaten the fruit, they felt ashamed. They hid from God because they were afraid. Then God said to them:

God: You have eaten the fruit of the tree from which I told you not to.

Adam: The woman gave it to me, and so I ate it.

God: Why did you do such a thing?

Eve: The serpent tricked me into it.

Reader 9: Then God said to the serpent:

God: I will put hatred between you and the woman, between your followers and her offspring.

Reader 10: To Adam and Eve God said:

God: Because of your sin the ground is cursed. You must labor hard until the day you die. You are dirt and to dirt you will return.

Reader 11: Then God put Adam and Eve out of the garden.

adapted from Genesis 2 and 3

We Remember

How was grace lost for all?
Grace was lost for all through the sin of our first parents.

Who overcame sin so we could have the gift of grace?
Jesus overcame sin so we could have the gift of grace.

We Respond

I will thank Jesus for the gift of grace. When I find it hard to do something good, I will pray, "Jesus, help me."

FAMILY CORNER

God created us to share his life and live with him forever. Pondering Scripture helps us appreciate God's goodness and shun sin.

Read
2 Corinthians 6:1–2

Discuss
- How can we make something good out of our sufferings?
- What does our family do to show we appreciate God's grace?

Pray
My Jesus, mercy!

Do
- Analyze several television commercials. Discuss what values are stressed and the true value of the things advertised. What claims are exaggerated?
- Share with your children your struggle to resist buying things you do not need. Discuss the intangible things your family has that do not cost money.
- Evaluate your family rules. How does each one promote happy family living?
- Why are family values important?
- Visit church to tell God you want to praise him in all you do. Decide on a special way to show your love.
- Why does the Church call the sin of Adam and Eve a "happy fault"?

❏ Signature

101

17 God Sent His Son Jesus to Live among Us

God Prepared a People and a Mother for the Savior

When something important is going to happen, we prepare for it. How does your family prepare for Christmas?

One of the most important things that ever happened was the coming of Jesus on the first Christmas. Do you remember how God prepared the world for his Son? First, God chose people from whom the Savior would come. He called Abraham to be the father of these people. God led them to know and love him.

When God's people were slaves in Egypt, God called Moses to free them and lead them to the Promised Land. He made a covenant of love with them and gave them his laws. Then God gave his people kings, like David. When the people forgot their covenant, God sent prophets to call them back to him.

Finally, God chose Mary to be the Mother of Jesus. God kept her free from original sin. He sent an angel to announce that she would be the Mother of the Savior. Mary listened to God's message and said yes. When she and Joseph were married, Joseph became the foster father of God's own Son.

When Mary said yes, the Son of God became man through the power of the Holy Spirit.

Circle the names of people on this page who had a role in preparing for the Savior.

Jesus Was Born in a Stable in Bethlehem

According to God's plan, Caesar, the Roman emperor, ordered a census. The head of each family had to register in his home town.

Joseph was from the family of David. He had to travel from Nazareth to Bethlehem, the town of David. He went with Mary, his wife, who was soon to have a child. Joseph and Mary stayed in a stable because there was no room for them in the inn. While they were there, Mary gave birth to a son. She wrapped him in swaddling clothes and laid him in a manger.

There were shepherds nearby, keeping watch over their flocks through the night. The angel of the Lord appeared to them. The glory of the Lord shone around them. They were very much afraid, but the angel said, "Do not be afraid. I bring you good news of great joy that will be for all the people. Today in the city of David a savior has been born for you. He is Christ the Lord. And here is a sign for you: you will find a baby wrapped in swaddling clothes and lying in a manger."

Suddenly, there was with the angel a great number of heavenly spirits. They were praising God and saying: "Glory to God in the highest, and peace to his people on earth."

The shepherds hurried away and found Mary and Joseph, and the baby lying in a manger. They told what they had seen and heard. Then they praised God.

adapted from Luke 2:1–20

Christmas Word Search

Circle the words in the puzzle. Check them by the crown as you find them.

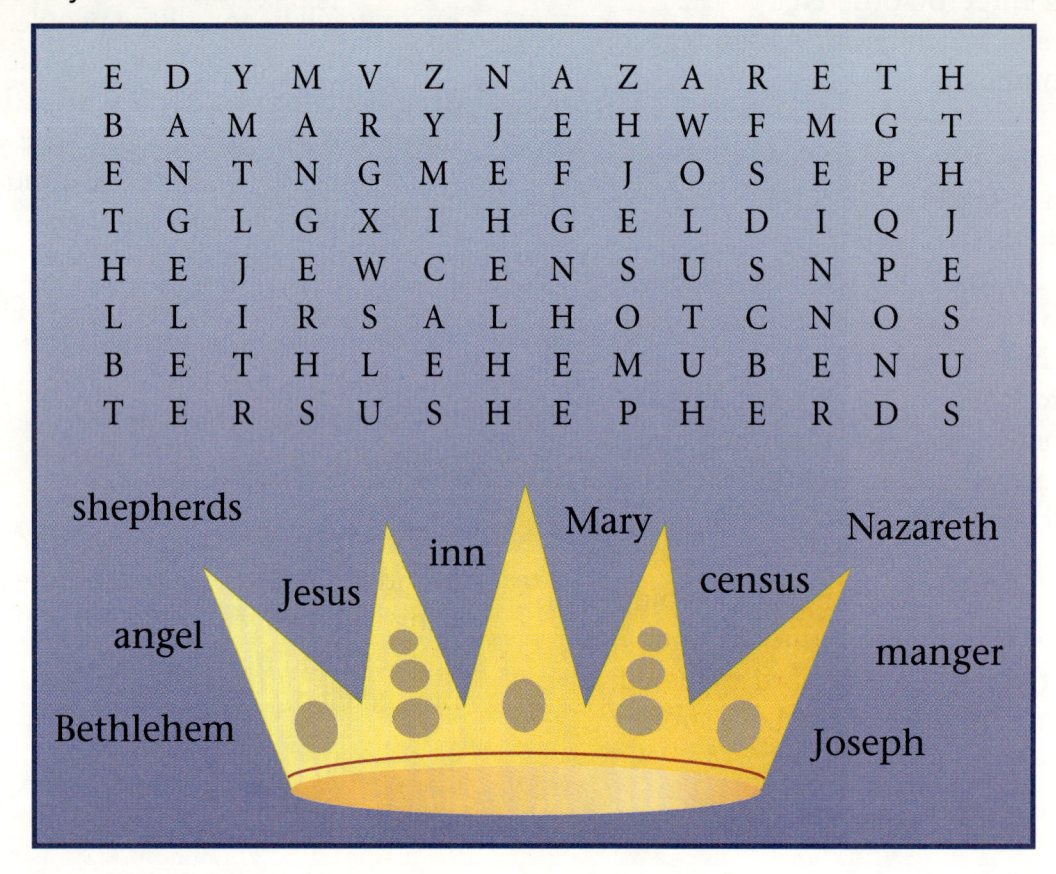

```
E D Y M V Z N A Z A R E T H
B A M A R Y J E H W F M G T
E N T N G M E F J O S E P H
T G L G X I H G E L D I Q J
H E J E W C E N S U S N P E
L L I R S A L H O T C N O S
B E T H L E H E M U B E N U
T E R S U S H E P H E R D S
```

shepherds
Jesus
inn
Mary
census
Nazareth
angel
manger
Bethlehem
Joseph

Find the word that matches the clue. Print it neatly on the line.

1. Mother of Jesus _____

2. Foster father of Jesus _____

3. Our Savior's name _____

4. One who announced the birth of Jesus _____

5. Holy Family's first visitors _____

6. Place where Mary laid Jesus _____

7. Place that had no room for Mary and Joseph _____

8. Reason Mary and Joseph went to Bethlehem _____

9. City of David _____

10. Town where Joseph and Mary lived _____

104

Simeon Recognized Jesus as the Light of the World

Jesus came as a light to lead all people back to God. He came to overcome the darkness of sin and to teach us truth.

Mary and Joseph took the child Jesus to the Temple to present him to the Lord. An old man named Simeon knew the child was the light of the world. He was happy that he had lived to see the Savior.

Simeon took Jesus into his arms and praised God, saying:

> "Now, Lord, you can let your servant die in peace. You have kept your word. My eyes have seen the salvation which you have prepared for all peoples to see. He is a light to reveal you to everyone. He is the glory of your people Israel."
> adapted from Luke 2:29–32

Simeon told Mary that she would have much sorrow. Her son Jesus would suffer and die in his battle against evil. Mary would share in his sufferings.

If we choose to follow Jesus, it will not always be easy. Jesus told his followers that they would sometimes suffer for doing the things he taught them.

Jesus Lived a Hidden Life

The Bible tells us very little about the years when Jesus was growing up. These years in Nazareth are called the **hidden life** of Jesus.

The people of Nazareth did not know that Jesus was the Savior, the Son of God. Jesus lived as any other Jewish boy. He was obedient and respectful to his parents and teachers. He played with the other boys. He was kind and helpful to his neighbors. People knew him only as the son of Joseph and Mary. Jesus probably worked as a carpenter like Joseph until he was about thirty years old.

We learn an important truth from the hidden life of Jesus: through our ordinary actions we can give God our worship and love. We join our actions with those of Jesus and offer them to God. Then even our most ordinary actions become pleasing to God.

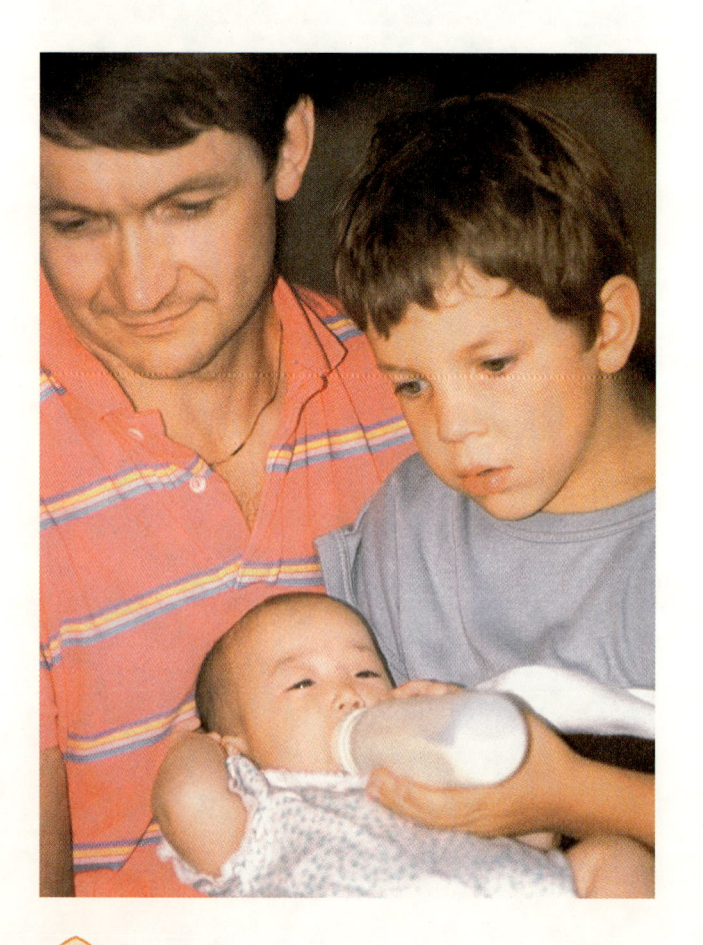

Jesus Is Our Light

> "I am the light of the world. Whoever follows me will not walk in darkness, but will have the light of life."
>
> John 8:12

We are followers of Jesus. We follow his light. We can help to make his light burn brightly wherever we are. We can make his light burn brightly in our own homes. Each member of a family can make Christ's light shine. Then everyone will see that Jesus is Lord of that family!

God our Father gave us the fourth commandment to help us make Jesus the Lord of our families. It tells us, "Honor your father and your mother."

Use the code key to find five words that tell us how we honor our parents.

$\underline{}\ \underline{}\ \underline{V}\ \underline{}\quad \underline{}\ \underline{B}\ \underline{}\ \underline{}$
2 3   1   3   1 8

$\underline{H}\ \underline{}\ \underline{}\ \underline{}\ \underline{}\ \underline{A}\ \underline{}$
    1 2 4   4 5   8

$\underline{}\ \underline{}\ \underline{}\ \underline{}\ \underline{}\ \underline{C}\ \underline{}$
5 1 6 4 1   7

Code Key							
1	2	3	4	5	6	7	8
E	L	O	P	R	S	T	Y

Others besides our parents guide and protect us. When we respect and obey our leaders, we keep the fourth commandment and make Christ's light burn brightly.

Light the Candles

Put a flame and ☧ on the candle if the sentence is about making the light of Christ burn more brightly.

1 Tom thanks Mom and Dad for the happy birthday celebration.

2 Sarah complains because she has to help with the dishes.

3 Anna, Pete, and their family pray together before the children go to bed.

4 Susan practices her flute because she knows her dad works hard to pay for her lessons.

5 Juan helps his dad in the yard so they can have time to play ball together.

6 Brad shouts in anger because his dad took him to soccer practice late.

A Puzzle for You!

Fill in the boxes with the letters of the missing words in each sentence.

1. Jesus shows us the way to eternal _____ .
2. Jesus overcame the darkness of _____ .
3. Simeon said Jesus was the _____ of his people.
4. To follow Jesus is sometimes _____ .
5. Jesus came to teach all people the _____ .

We Remember

What mystery occurred at the Annunciation?
At the Annunciation, the Son of God became man through the power of the Holy Spirit.

How do we honor our parents?
We honor our parents when we love, obey, help, respect, and pray for them.

We Respond

I believe in Jesus Christ, the Son of God, who was born of the Virgin Mary!

I will keep the light of Christ burning brightly by obeying without complaining.

FAMILY CORNER

The Incarnation is the great mystery of the Son of God's becoming man. Jesus came to earth to save us and show us the way to heaven.

Read
Luke 2:8–14

Discuss
- What was the message the angel gave to the shepherds?
- How did the other angels praise God?
- In what ways can we help spread the Good News of Jesus' coming?
- How does Jesus live among us today?

Pray
Thank you, Jesus, for becoming like us. Help us to be like you.

Do
- Sing or pray together the "Glory to God" from the Mass.
- Have each family member read about the Christmas customs of a different country. During a meal, or at another time, share what you have learned.
- Do something as a family to help someone less fortunate than you.
- Keep Christ in Christmas by setting up a crib scene.
- Talk about the light of Christ. Have a candle on the table during supper. Ask yourself what you have done to make the light of Christ burn more brightly in your family.

❏ Signature

We Celebrate Jesus, Who Is Our Light

Song

Introduction

Leader 1: Jesus is our light. He shows us the way to his Father. At Baptism he placed his own light within us. He tells us to let his light shine through us everywhere we go. He wants us to take his light to people who do not know him. Let us tell God of our joy. Let us celebrate!

Prayer

All: God our Father, all light comes from you. You fill with light the hearts of all who believe in your Son. May we celebrate his love and his presence now and forever. We ask this in Jesus' name. Amen.

Readings

Leader 2: Our first reading is from the Gospel of St. John. Jesus had gone to the Temple to celebrate a special feast. Four large lamps were lighted. Their light spread out over the city of Jerusalem. Jesus spoke about himself.

Reader 1: I am the light of the world. Whoever follows me will not walk in darkness, but will have the light of life.

John 8:12

The Gospel of the Lord.

All: Praise to you, Lord Jesus Christ!

Leader 3: Our second reading is from a letter of St. Paul. He tells us how to live as children of light.

Reader 2: You were once darkness, but now you are light in the Lord. Live as children of light. The light of Christ will be seen in your goodness. Try to learn what the Lord wants you to do. Have nothing to do with sin and darkness.

adapted from Ephesians 5:8–11

The Word of the Lord.

All: Thanks be to God.

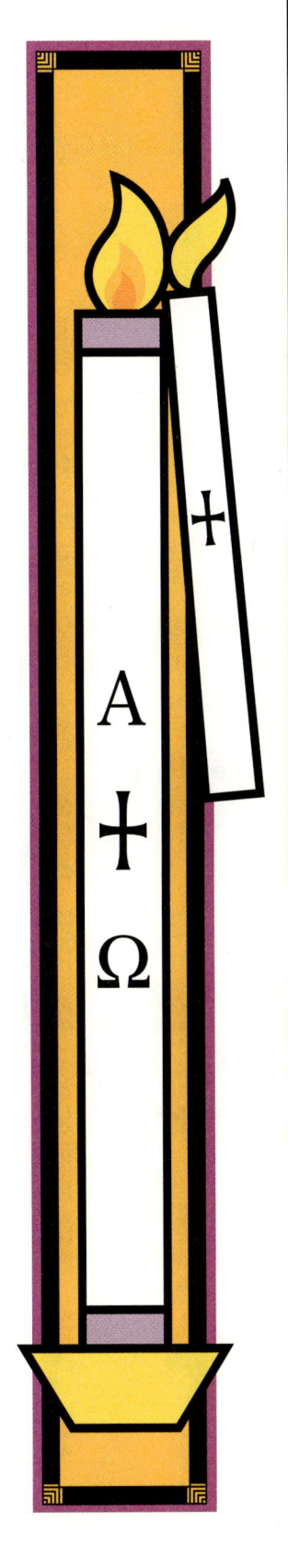

Response to the Readings

Antiphon

Let us walk with joy in the light of the Lord!

Leader 4: Lord Jesus, you have filled our souls with the light of faith in Baptism. We thank and praise you. We want to live always in your light.

All: (Repeat antiphon.)

Leader 5: Lord Jesus, you told us to let our light shine for others to see. Then they too will come to the Father and give him praise. Help us to shine with the light of your goodness at home, in school, and with our friends.

All: (Repeat antiphon.)

Leader 6: Lord Jesus, you ask missionaries to take your light to people who do not know you. Fill them with your light. Help them to show those people how much you love them. We cannot go to faraway places, but we want to help the missionaries by our prayers and sacrifices.

All: (Repeat antiphon.)

Offering (*Prayers and sacrifices may be brought to the table.*)

Leader 7: Jesus is our light. Let us think of the good things Jesus did in his life. His example is a light for us. Let us ask Jesus to help us to be like him.
(*Pause for silent prayer.*)

Prayer

All: Father, we share the light of your Son, Jesus. Remind us always that his love and his light are in us. Teach us to keep his light burning brightly and to share it with others. We ask this in Jesus' name. Amen.

Song

18 Jesus Revealed the Kingdom of God

Jesus Begins His Public Mission

John the Baptist was sent by God to prepare people to receive Jesus and the kingdom of God.

Many people came to hear John preach and were baptized in the Jordan River. John's baptism of these people was not the Sacrament of Baptism as we know it. It was a baptism of sorrow for sin.

When Jesus left Nazareth to begin teaching, he came to John to be baptized. Jesus was the all-holy Son of God. He did not need to be baptized. By being baptized, Jesus showed that he made himself one with sinners.

Jesus' baptism by John was also a sign that he was giving his life to the work his Father had sent him to do. With his baptism Jesus began his public **mission** as the **Messiah,** the Savior.

The Baptism of Jesus

Narrator: Jesus came to the Jordan River, where John was baptizing people. He went down into the water to be baptized, but John tried to stop him.

John: Do you come to me to be baptized? I need to be baptized by you.

Jesus: Let us do this to fulfill what God wants.

Narrator: So John baptized Jesus. Then God gave a sign of his love and approval of Jesus. As Jesus came out of the water, the heavens opened. The Spirit of God came down like a dove upon him. A voice came from heaven:

Voice of God: This is my beloved Son. I am well pleased with him.

adapted from Matthew 3:13–17

Prepare the Lord's Way in Your Heart

Column 1 tells how some children need to change.
Column 2 has messages John the Baptist might have for them.

Print the letter of the message that helps each child prepare for God's kingdom.

_____ 1. Su Lin will not let Jimmy play on her team because Jimmy isn't a good player.

_____ 2. Anna goes to her room and listens to her CDs when it's time to do the dishes.

_____ 3. Ron has toys and games he hardly uses. Now he wants a new, expensive toy.

_____ 4. Bill makes few mistakes in his schoolwork. He laughs when others make them.

_____ 5. Jane complains when her mother serves some foods.

A. Help others instead of hurting their feelings.
B. Be satisfied with what you have. Give money to the missions to feed starving children.
C. Winning isn't everything. It's more important to be kind to others than to win a game.
D. Be grateful for having good meals to eat. Thank your mother and eat everything she prepares.
E. Be a good family member. Help out cheerfully.

Jesus Showed His Power over Satan

After his baptism Jesus was led by the Holy Spirit into the desert. For forty days he fasted and prayed in order to prepare to do his Father's work.

Satan saw that Jesus was weak from hunger. He tempted Jesus to turn away from God's plan. He tempted Jesus to work wonders and make a great kingdom on earth. Then people would believe he was the Messiah. Satan also showed Jesus all the kingdoms that he could rule if he would worship Satan.

Jesus answered Satan's temptations by showing love for his Father. Jesus chose to obey his Father's plan.

Satan always tries to destroy our friendship with God. He tries to draw us away from doing God's will. God does not force us to love him. He leaves us free. But God helps us overcome temptation if we ask him.

Find some acts in the box that help you overcome temptation. Color their spaces yellow.

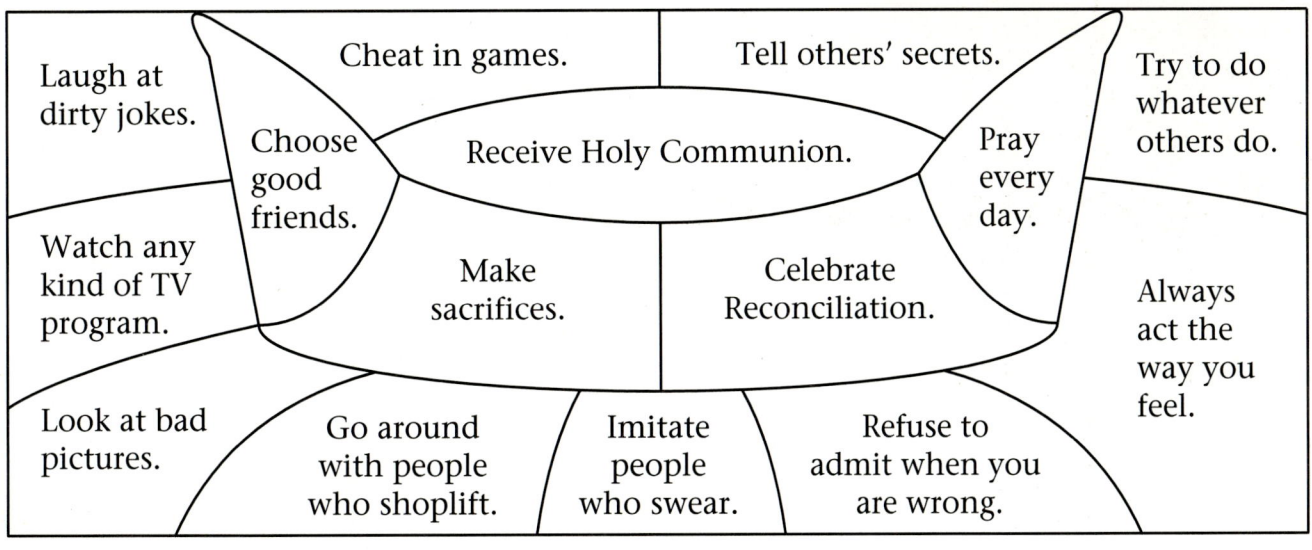

- Laugh at dirty jokes.
- Cheat in games.
- Tell others' secrets.
- Try to do whatever others do.
- Choose good friends.
- Receive Holy Communion.
- Pray every day.
- Watch any kind of TV program.
- Make sacrifices.
- Celebrate Reconciliation.
- Always act the way you feel.
- Look at bad pictures.
- Go around with people who shoplift.
- Imitate people who swear.
- Refuse to admit when you are wrong.

Jesus Showed His Power over Satan

113

Jesus Worked Miracles to Show the Kingdom Had Come

Jesus performed special works as signs that he had brought God's kingdom to earth. The Gospel calls these wonderful deeds of Jesus **miracles,** or signs. Jesus' miracles helped people believe that he was the Messiah.

Some miracles showed power over nature. Jesus calmed storms at sea. Jesus also drove evil spirits out of people. His power over demons was a sign that he was the Savior who would overcome evil. Wherever Jesus rules, sin is driven out. Jesus brings his goodness, love, and happiness to those who open their hearts to him.

Jesus Told Parables about the Kingdom of God

Jesus revealed the kingdom of God in his preaching. He taught by **parables,** or stories. In his parables Jesus compared the kingdom of God to everyday things the people saw or did. The parables made them think.

Have you ever seen a mustard seed? Jesus told a parable about this seed:

> "The kingdom of God is like a mustard seed, which is the smallest of all seeds. . . . But it grows to become the largest of plants, sending out branches for the birds of the sky to live in its shade."
>
> adapted from Mark 4:30–32

Jesus was telling the people that God's kingdom would begin small but would grow into something great. The Church belongs to the kingdom of God. People of every nation have become members of the Church. When we pray, make sacrifices, and love as Jesus did, the Church grows.

Jesus also told a parable about the great value of God's kingdom:

> "The kingdom of God is like a buyer looking for fine pearls. When he finds a pearl of great price, he sells all that he has and buys it."
>
> adapted from Matthew 13:45–46

God's kingdom within us is the life of grace. It is such a priceless gift that we could never pay enough to get it. To keep it safe is worth any sacrifice. God's kingdom is also in heaven. No earthly treasure can compare with what God has for us there.

Fill in the missing words.

Jesus taught using stories called __ __ __ __ __ __ __ __ .

He told us that God's kingdom grows like a __ __ __ __ __ __ __ seed.

The kingdom of God is like a fine __ __ __ __ __ .

115

We Spread God's Kingdom in Different Ways

Then she was called "Sister Clare" and lived in a convent. She spent her whole life praying, fasting, and working for the love of God and for the spread of God's kingdom.

A legend tells of a miracle, a sign of God's love for Clare. One Christmas Eve, Clare was sick in bed and could not go to the chapel for Mass. Yet somehow she saw the Mass and heard the music and singing. That is why St. Clare is called the patron saint of television.

We can ask St. Clare to pray for us that we will use all things in a way that will lead us to God.

The Story of St. Clare

Clare was born into a wealthy family in Assisi. She was very beautiful and gentle. The finest young men of the town wanted to marry her. But Clare had met Francis of Assisi and wanted to love God as he did. Like Francis, she was joyful and loved everything God had made.

Clare liked to be alone to think of God. She wanted to give her life to God. She gladly gave up all she had in her beautiful home. In the chapel of St. Mary of the Angels, Clare offered her life to God. St. Francis cut her golden hair and gave her the poor clothing of a Franciscan.

Good Christians love and serve God in all they do. With their talents they bring God's love to others in many ways. They bring the Spirit of Jesus to whatever they do. Can you tell how these people are spreading God's kingdom?

Keys to the Kingdom

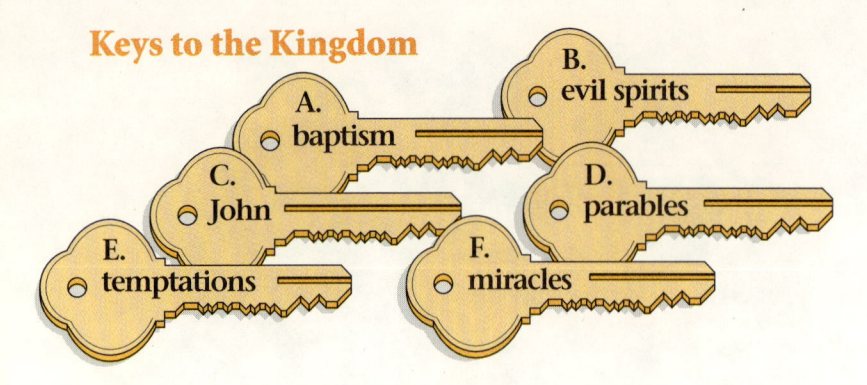

A. baptism
B. evil spirits
C. John
D. parables
E. temptations
F. miracles

Find the answer to each question in a key and write its letter on the line.

_____ 1. What were the stories Jesus told about the kingdom?

_____ 2. What were the signs Jesus worked to show the kingdom had come?

_____ 3. What did Jesus show power over as a sign that his kingdom of goodness will win?

_____ 4. What was a sign that Jesus was starting his public mission?

_____ 5. How did Satan try to draw Jesus away from God's plan?

_____ 6. Who baptized Jesus?

We Remember

What must we do to receive the kingdom of God in our hearts?
To receive the kingdom of God in our hearts, we must give up our selfish ways.

How can we help the Church grow?
We can help the Church grow by praying, making sacrifices, and loving as Jesus did.

Words to Know
mission   Messiah
miracle   parable

We Respond

Jesus, I want to prepare for your kingdom. Help me to be more loving and unselfish.

FAMILY CORNER

The parables of Jesus shed light on the kingdom of God. We can work to spread this kingdom, especially by choosing what is right.

Read
Matthew 13:44–46

Discuss
- Why did the man sell all that he had in order to buy the field?
- Why did the merchant sell what he owned in order to buy just one pearl?
- What does God expect us to do in order to gain the kingdom of heaven?

Pray
Your kingdom come!

Do
- Discuss how members of the family can become better members of the kingdom of God.
- Evaluate your family's use of television. Discuss whether the programs we watch make us better people and which programs we should stop watching.
- Plan a family mission project to help spread the kingdom to faraway places.

❏ Signature

19 Jesus Came to Give Life

Jesus Cured the Leper

In the time of Jesus, no one wanted to go near those who had leprosy because they were afraid of the sickness. Lepers often had to leave their homes and live apart from other people.

> One day a leper came to Jesus and knelt before him. "Lord," he begged, "if you want to, you can cure me."
> Moved with pity, Jesus stretched out his hand and touched him. "I will do it," he said. "Be cured!" At once the leprosy left the man, and he was cured.
> adapted from Mark 1:40–42

The Gospel tells us that Jesus cured many lepers. Then they could begin a new life among their people. What Jesus did for lepers is a sign of what he wants to do for us. Jesus came to heal us of the sickness of sin. He came to bring us the new life of grace and to make us one in his family—the Church.

Sin is like leprosy. It takes us away from God and others. It weakens us. It makes us less able to use our gifts for the good of God's family.

In the Sacrament of Reconciliation, Jesus heals us of sin by forgiving us. When we bring our sins to him and ask his pardon and help, he makes us one with God and one another.

How Do Our Sins Hurt Others?

Draw a line from the sin in column 1 to the hurt it caused in column 2 to see how sin hurts people.

1. When Jerry told a lie,
2. Because Maria was unkind to her sister,
3. When Bart lost his temper,
4. Because Steve used his friend's bike without asking,
5. Although no one knows about the sin Ann committed,

- the little girl's feelings were hurt.
- her shame makes her less loving and kind.
- his friend had no way to get to his game.
- his friend was blamed unfairly for something.
- he got into a fight and hurt another boy.

How Can We Give Jesus' Healing Love?

Read each sentence in column 1 about people who needed Jesus' healing love. Find the sentence in column 2 that tells who gave them this love. Put the letter of that sentence on the line in column 1.

_____ 1. Tony's team lost its game.

_____ 2. Mary was sick and couldn't go skating with her friends.

_____ 3. Mother was very tired from preparing supper after she had worked all day.

_____ 4. Mr. Garcia was very sad when his mother died.

_____ 5. Robert got bad grades in spelling.

A. Betty and Sandy made her a get-well card.
B. Tom studied with him until his work improved.
C. Jerry told him how sorry he felt and gave the man a comforting hug.
D. Tom made sure he told his friend how well he had played.
E. The twins offered to do the dishes after supper.

Jesus Brought Life to the Widow's Son

Jesus was on his way to the city of Nain with his disciples. As they came near the city gate, a dead man was being carried out. He was an only son, and his mother was a widow.

Jesus' heart was filled with pity for this mother. "Do not cry," he said to her. Then he touched the coffin, and those carrying the body stopped. Jesus said, "Young man, I tell you, arise!" The dead man sat up and began to speak. Jesus gave him back to his mother.

Everyone was filled with awe and praised God, saying, "God has visited his people."

adapted from Luke 7:11–16

Something to Think About

How strong is my faith? Do I think of Jesus and turn to him for help when I need it?

Check the ending that tells how Jesus will probably help in these situations.

1. When I must do something hard, Jesus will

   _____ change things so that I do not have to do what is hard.

   _____ give me the courage to do what is right, even if it is hard.

2. When I have a problem to solve, Jesus will

   _____ make things work out so that I get what I want.

   _____ help me to make the right choice and carry it out.

3. When I am disappointed, Jesus will

   _____ help me to accept things as they are and still be happy.

   _____ take away what has disappointed me.

4. When I study the mysteries of faith, Jesus will

   _____ help me to understand them completely.

   _____ help me to believe even what I do not fully understand.

The Cure of the Blind Man

Reader 1: The signs Jesus worked showed that the kingdom of God had come.

Reader 2: As Jesus came to Jericho, a blind beggar was sitting at the side of the road. He could hear that a crowd was passing by.

Blind Man: What is happening?

Man: Jesus of Nazareth is passing by.

Blind Man: Jesus, Son of David, have pity on me!

Crowd: Be quiet! Don't make a scene!

Reader 3: But the blind man would not be quiet. He only cried out all the more.

Blind Man: Jesus, Son of David, help me. Have pity on me!

Reader 4: Jesus heard the blind man shouting to him. He stopped and stood still.

Jesus: Bring the blind man here to me.

Reader 5: They led the blind man to Jesus.

Jesus: What do you want me to do for you?

Blind Man: Lord, please let me see!

Jesus: Have sight. Your faith has saved you.

Reader 6: That very moment, the man was able to see. He began to follow Jesus, giving glory to God.

Blind Man: Praise God! I can see! I can see!

Crowd: Praise God!

adapted from Luke 18:35–43

Think: Do you *see* chances each day to live as a child of God's kingdom?

The Cure of the Deaf Man

Reader 1: Jesus came to the Ten Cities. Some people brought him a deaf man who spoke unclearly.

People: Lord, please lay your hands on him. He cannot hear or speak well.

Reader 2: Jesus took the man off by himself, away from the crowd. He put his fingers into the man's ears. He touched the man's tongue. Then Jesus looked up to heaven and groaned.

Jesus: Be opened!

Reader 3: At once the man's ears were opened, and he could hear. He began to speak clearly too.

People: Listen! The man is speaking! He can hear!

Jesus: None of you must say anything about this.

Reader 4: But the people were too amazed to remain quiet. They spoke more and more of the wonderful things they had seen.

People: Jesus of Nazareth has cured the deaf man! He has done wonders! He has made the deaf hear and the silent speak!

adapted from Mark 7:31–37

Think: Do you *hear* God speak to you through people and things that happen?

Something to Do

Work the puzzle. It tells what Mary the Mother of Jesus said to do when God speaks to you. On each blank, print the letter that comes before the one below it.

__ __   __ __ __ __ __ __ __ __   __ __
E P   X I B U F W F S   I F

__ __ __ __ __   __ __ __ __.
U F M M T   Z P V

124

Complete the sentences, using the words in the Word Bank.

1. The miracles of Jesus show he was the _____.

2. Just as he healed from leprosy, Jesus heals from _____.

3. We need open ears to hear God's _____.

4. Jesus healed the blind and deaf men because of their _____.

5. Jesus gave back _____ to the widow's son.

Word Bank
life sin faith
Word Messiah

We Remember

What did Jesus say about anyone who believes in him?

Jesus said,
 "I am the resurrection and the life; whoever believes in me, even if he dies, will live."

John 11:25–26

We Respond

"Lord, I have come to believe that you are the Messiah, the Son of God."

John 11:27

FAMILY CORNER

The miracles of Jesus are signs of his love and his power to overcome sin and bring us to eternal life. We can be instruments of Jesus' healing power by reflecting his love in our words and deeds.

Read
Luke 7:18–23

Discuss
- To whom were John's disciples referring when they asked, "Are you the one who is to come?"
- Did Jesus answer their question? Was he the one whom they were expecting?
- What were some miracles Jesus performed?
- Does God still work miracles today?

Pray
If you want to, you can cure us. Come, Lord Jesus, come!

Do
- Make a family statement of faith, a creed. Let everyone mention something a Catholic believes about God the Father, Son, Holy Spirit, and about the Church.
- Plan to celebrate the Sacrament of Reconciliation as a family. Prepare at home together for the sacrament. Include some sign that each family member is sorry for hurting another.
- Plan as a family to brighten the day of someone who is sad.

❏ Signature

20 God's Kingdom Is a Kingdom of Love

Jesus Taught Us about the Spirit of the Kingdom

Jesus taught us that the spirit of God's kingdom is a spirit of generous, loving service. God's plan is for us to love one another.

Read the following teachings of Jesus and think about them. Write the number of the message that matches each sentence in the box.

1. "You know that the law says, 'You shall not kill.' But I tell you this: You shall not be angry with your brother at all. If you are bringing your gift to the altar and remember that your brother has something against you, go first and make up with your brother. Then come and offer your gift."

   adapted from Matthew 5:21–24

2. "If someone tells you to carry a load for one mile, offer to carry it for two miles. And if someone asks for something from you, give him what he asks. Do not turn your back on a person who wants to borrow from you."

   adapted from Matthew 5:41–42

3. "Love your enemies. Pray for people who do you wrong. In this way you will be children of your heavenly Father. He makes the sun rise on the bad and the good. Be perfect, just as your heavenly Father is perfect. Do to others whatever you would like them to do to you."
adapted from Matthew 5:44–48; 7:12

_____ Share generously what you have.

_____ Forgive those who hurt you.

_____ Be kind and courteous to everyone.

A Check for Service

Read these sentences. Check (✓) each one that tells a way to spread God's kingdom by serving and loving others.

_____ 1. Work hard so you can use your talents to make others happy.

_____ 2. Pray for the needs of others.

_____ 3. Make others feel they are not as good as you are.

_____ 4. Refuse to join others in looking at bad pictures.

_____ 5. Offer your help even before you are asked.

_____ 6. Boss others around.

_____ 7. Sacrifice some of your money to give to the missions.

_____ 8. Act as if you are better than someone else.

_____ 9. Do jobs at home and school carefully and cheerfully.

_____ 10. Do something to cheer up someone who is sick or lonely.

Checking Up on the Unit
Check the right ending for each sentence.

1. God created human beings because

   ____ he wanted to share his life and happiness with them.

   ____ he needed them for his happiness.

2. After Adam and Eve sinned,

   ____ God no longer loved them.

   ____ God still loved them and promised to help them.

3. The Redeemer whom God sent

   ____ was his own Son born of the Virgin Mary.

   ____ had to be baptized because of his sin.

4. The special signs Jesus worked to reveal the kingdom of God are called

   ____ parables.

   ____ miracles.

5. By healing the sick, Jesus showed that he had come to

   ____ rid the world of sickness and pain.

   ____ heal people of the sickness of sin.

6. Jesus worked miracles to

   ____ reveal that he was the Messiah.

   ____ force people to believe in him.

7. Some people did not believe in Jesus because they were expecting

   ____ a spiritual kingdom.

   ____ an earthly Messiah.

What's the Parable?
Write the answers to the questions on the lines.

1. In which parable did Jesus say that the kingdom of God would be small at first but would grow into something great?

   _____

2. In which parable did Jesus teach us that God's kingdom is more valuable than anything else?

   _____

Who's Who?
Write the letter of the answer on each line.

- A. blind man
- B. the leper
- C. deaf man
- D. John the Baptist
- E. Satan
- F. Jesus

_____ 1. Which man had a sickness that was a symbol of sin?

_____ 2. Which man called out for help and was cured at once by Jesus?

_____ 3. Which man did Jesus cure at the request of others?

_____ 4. Who tried to turn Jesus away from doing his Father's will?

_____ 5. Who taught that serving God means obeying his laws with a true and generous love?

_____ 6. Who told the people to change their hearts and prepare for the coming of the kingdom of God?

Word Find
Find words that name things you can use to help spread God's kingdom. (Words go across and down.) Circle them and be ready to tell how you could use each one to help and serve others.

```
P T R P O S K A T E S
E I B I K E N B O O K
A M I C I T O Y S M T
C E A L L O W A N C E
E F O O D O L L S W P
G R N T A L E N T S A
A V T H R S D J O Y P
M O N E Y Z G H O M E
E Y E S O T E F U N R
```

Who's Who in Your Life?
List some of the people who have brought you closer to Jesus.

_____

_____

_____

_____

Planning to Grow
Think of Jesus, the light of the world. He wants you to please his Father and help spread his light all over the world.

Write two ways you plan to do this.

1. _____

2. _____

FAMILY CORNER

God's kingdom is already on earth when we try to love and serve others as Jesus calls us to do.

Read
Matthew 5:44–48

Discuss
- What things would change in our world if everyone did what Jesus tells us to do?
- How can we do good to those who persecute us?
- How do you wish others to treat you?

Pray
Jesus, gentle and humble of heart, make my heart like yours!

Do
- Say something nice to a person who doesn't seem to like you.
- Take time to share with one another how thoughtful acts make you feel.
- As a family project, assist a person in a nursing home, prison, or refugee center.

❏ Signature

We Pray for the Coming of God's Kingdom

Song

Leader: God invites all of us to live in his kingdom. If we believe in Jesus and open our hearts to his works, he will free us from the power of sin. He will give us peace and joy in this life. He will bring us to the kingdom of his Father, where we will enjoy eternal life. Let us listen to what Jesus tells us to do.

Reader 1: Give to anyone who asks and, if anyone wants to borrow, do not turn away.

Reader 2: Love your enemies.

Reader 3: Pray for people who hurt you.

Reader 4: Do to others what you would like them to do to you.

adapted from Matthew 5:44; 7:12

All: Jesus, gentle and humble of heart, make our hearts like yours!

Leader: Lord, we have heard your Word. Help us to accept it and show our love by what we do.

Song

Presentation of Gifts

(Place your promise of good deeds on the table as a sign that you want to follow Jesus.)

Leader: God our Father, we have praised you in song and prayer. We have shown that we want to serve you in all our brothers and sisters. Help us do this today and every day.

All: Amen.

Song

Color a cross when you make a sacrifice to bring God's kingdom here.

FAMILY FEATURE

A Family Candle

Prema and her family live in India where each year the Hindus celebrate a marvelous festival of lights called Diwali (dee WAH lee). For this day they clean their houses from top to bottom. They make clay pots and fill them with oil. These lamps are lighted and set along the walkways, streets, porches, and yards. In the evening they are a glorious sight. The Hindus light the way to their homes in hopes that the goddess Lackshmi will visit them. Catholics in India have adopted the feast and celebrate Christ as the Light of the World on that day. They set out lamps and celebrate Mass.

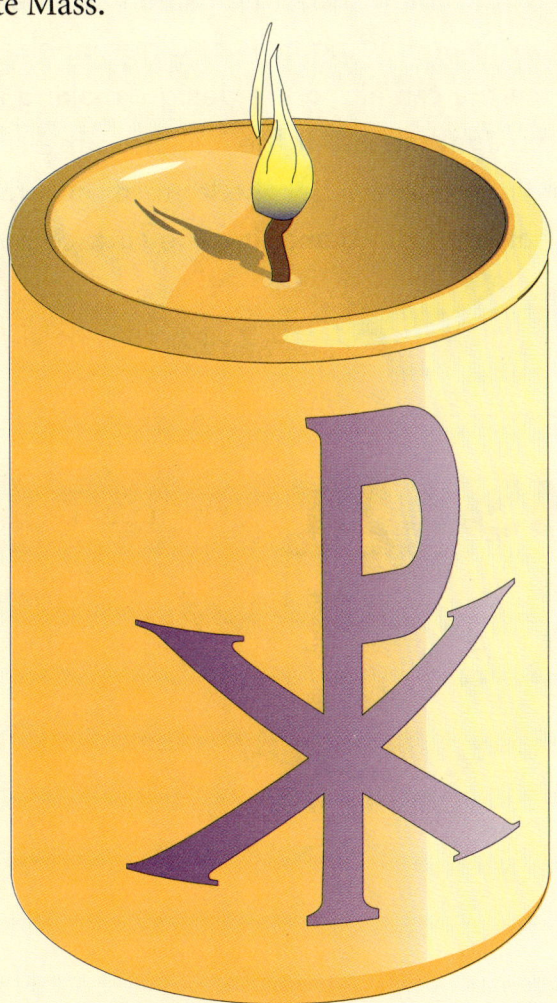

You might wish to make a special Christ candle to light on festive occasions. Purchase a large candle and decorate it with a symbol for Christ, choosing from those on this page. Keep it in your prayer corner but then set it in a centerpiece of flowers on your table on special days such as baptismal anniversaries, Easter, Christmas, or Candlemas Day on February 2.

You might prefer to make a tin lantern. Clean a tin can and remove the paper label and glue. (Pineapple cans are good because they seldom have sharp edges.) Fill the can with water and freeze it. Then draw a design on the can using a marker, or draw a design on paper and secure the paper to the can with rubber bands. Lay the can on its side on newspapers or old towels and, using nails of different sizes and a hammer, pierce the can along the design, making a pattern of holes to let the light out. Melt the ice and put a candle stub or votive candle in the can. Set the lantern on something to prevent the hot can from damaging the surface it rests on.

Son of God

Use the code to discover some good advice. Talk about what it means to you.

0 = a	3 = e	6 = t	9 = u	12 = r	15 = n
1 = y	4 = s	7 = o	10 = k	13 = f	16 = w
2 = d	5 = h	8 = l	11 = p	14 = i	17 = c

__ __ __ __ __ __ __ __ __ __ __ __ __
10 3 3 11 1 7 9 12 13 0 17 3 6 7

__ __ __ __ __ __ __ __ __ __ __ __ __ __
 6 5 3 4 9 15 0 15 2 1 7 9 16 14 8 8

__ __ __ __ __ __ __ __ __ __ __ __ __ __!
15 7 6 4 3 3 6 5 3 4 5 0 2 7 16 4

(Answer: Keep your face to the sun and you will not see the shadows!)

Light of Christ

Act out a miracle or parable in which Jesus was light for us, or play charades. Conclude by singing "This Little Light of Mine."

Miracles

Wedding Feast at Cana *John 2:1–11*
Calming of the Storm *Matthew 8:23–27*
Multiplication of Loaves *John 6:1–15*
Large Catch of Fish *Luke 5:1–11*
Walking on the Sea *Mark 6:45–52*
Tax Money in the Fish *Matthew 17:24–27*
A Possessed Man *Mark 1:21–28*
Peter's Mother-in-Law *Matthew 8:14–15*
The Paralytic *Mark 2:1–12*
The Centurion's Servant *Matthew 8:5–13*
The Syrophoenician Woman *Mark 7:24–30*
The Blind Man *Luke 18:35–43*
The Widow's Son *Luke 7:11–17*
The Raising of Lazarus *John 11:1–44*

Parables

The Lost Sheep *Matthew 18:12–14*
The Lost Coin *Luke 15:8–10*
The Sower *Mark 4:2–9*
The Prodigal Son *Luke 15:11–32*
The Hidden Treasure *Matthew 13:44*
The Priceless Pearl *Matthew 13:45–46*
The Good Samaritan *Luke 10:25–37*
The Rich Man and Lazarus *Luke 16:19–31*
The House Built on Rock *Matthew 7:24–27*
The Two Sons *Matthew 21:28–32*
The Talents *Matthew 25:14–30*

Being Light

In the candle write or draw ways you can be light for your friends and neighbors.

Jesus Brings Us to the Kingdom of God

UNIT 5

The Paschal Mystery is central to our Christian faith. In this unit the children reflect on the suffering, death, resurrection, and ascension of Jesus. This enables them to enter more wholeheartedly into our celebration of the Eucharist and the feasts of the Church year. They learn about the fulfillment of Jesus' promise to send the Holy Spirit to help the Church know and love God and carry on his work. Then they rejoice with Mary, who was taken body and soul into heaven and crowned queen of heaven and earth.

21 Jesus Suffered and Died for Us

Jesus Was Honored as King

On the Sunday before he died, Jesus rode into Jerusalem. The people welcomed him as a king. They spread their clothes and palm branches on the road. They called him Son of David and shouted,

> "Hosanna! Blessed is he who comes in the name of the Lord!"
>
> Mark 11:9

The people thought Jesus would be the great leader who would free them from Roman rule. Jesus accepted the joyful praise of the people. This was his victory march. Soon he would win the victory over sin and death.

On Passion Sunday we carry blessed palms and proclaim that Jesus is King of heaven and earth. We greet him as the Redeemer who overcame sin and death by giving up his life and then rising to glory.

134

Jesus Made a New Covenant

At a Passover meal the Israelites celebrated how God had freed them from slavery in Egypt. They renewed their covenant by promising to keep God's commandments and to live as his chosen people. They offered a Passover lamb in sacrifice.

Jesus celebrated the Passover meal with his apostles the night before he died. At this meal Jesus made a New Covenant with them and us. He gave us a **new commandment.** He offered himself as the lamb who saves us from sin and death. By his power, bread and wine became his Body and Blood. He offered them to God as he would offer himself on the cross. Then he gave himself to his disciples under the forms of bread and wine.

This sacrifice offered by Jesus at the Last Supper was the first Mass. Now Jesus makes his sacrifice present in every Mass. The **Mass** is the sacrifice of the New Covenant. It is also our covenant meal celebrated and shared by God's holy people.

Write the law of the New Covenant by printing above each letter the one that comes before it in the alphabet.

__ __   __   __ __ __ __   __ __ __ __ __   __ __ __ ,
B T   J   I B W F   M P W F E   Z P V

__ __   __ __ __   __ __ __ __   __ __ __ __ __
T P   Z P V   B M T P   T I P V M E

__ __ __ __   __ __ __   __ __ __ __ __ __ .
M P W F   P O F   B O P U I F S

John 13:34

Jesus Faced His Agony

On the night before he died, Jesus went with Peter, James, and John to the garden of Gethsemane. He told them, "My soul is filled with sorrow. Wait here, and keep awake!"

Jesus was truly human. Like all people, he did not want to suffer or die. In fear he fell to the ground and prayed to his Father to save him from that hour. "My Father!" he said, "Everything is possible for you. Take this cup away from me. Still, let it be as you will, not as I will."

Jesus went back to the apostles, but they were asleep. He said to Peter, "Are you asleep? Couldn't you keep awake one hour with me? Watch and pray that you may not be put to the test." The apostles did not know what to say. Jesus left them and went away again to pray. He came back a second and a third time. Each time the apostles were sleeping. Then he said to them, "The hour has come. Get up! Let us go! My betrayer is near."

adapted from Mark 14:32–42

Jesus Gave His Life for Us

Reader 1: While Jesus was speaking to the apostles in the garden, Judas came with men armed with swords and clubs. He kissed Jesus as a sign that the men should capture him. They arrested Jesus, and the apostles ran away. Jesus was led to the high priest's house. There the high priest questioned Jesus.

Jesus: Why do you question me? Question those who heard me. They know what I have said.

Reader 2: One of the guards struck Jesus.

Guard 1: Is this the way you answer the high priest?

Reader 3: During the night the guards made fun of Jesus. They blindfolded him, hit him, and mocked him.

Guard 2: Play the prophet! Tell us who it was that hit you!

Reader 4: Jesus kept silent.

Reader 5: Early the next morning they bound Jesus and led him to Pontius Pilate, the Roman governor. The chief priests accused Jesus of many things.

Pilate: This man has done nothing that deserves death! I will have him whipped and then let him go.

Reader 6: So Pilate ordered Jesus to be whipped. The soldiers made a crown of thorns and placed it on his head. They threw a cloak about his shoulders and placed a reed in his hand. They knelt before him and struck him on the head with the reed.

Soldiers: Hail, King of the Jews!

Jesus Gave His Life for Us

Reader 7: Then Pilate had Jesus brought before the crowd in the courtyard.

Pilate: Behold the man!

Crowd: Crucify him! Crucify him!

Pilate: Why? What crime has he committed?

Reader 8: Pilate feared that a riot would begin. He took water and washed his hands as a sign that he would have nothing to do with this case.

Pilate: I find no guilt in him.

Reader 9: But Pilate handed Jesus over to be crucified. They led Jesus outside the gates of Jerusalem to a place called Calvary. They crucified him there. The people who passed by kept making fun of him.

People: Ha! Save yourself, if you are the Son of God, and come down from that cross!

Reader 10: The chief priests and scribes also joined in and mocked him.

Priests: He saved others, but he cannot save himself! Let him come down from the cross now. Then we will believe in him!

Reader 11: At noon, darkness fell over the whole land. At three o'clock, Jesus cried out with a loud voice.

Jesus: It is finished! Father, into your hands I entrust my spirit!

Reader 12: Then Jesus bowed his head and died. When the centurion guarding Jesus saw how he died, he was amazed.

Centurion: Truly this man was the Son of God!

adapted from Mark 15:1–47;
Luke 23:13–49; John 18:19–24; 19:5–6;
Matthew 27:15–44

We Take Up Our Cross

Jesus said that if we wish to follow him, we must take up our cross. This means accepting hard things that come into our lives. We may fail in things we try to do. Some people may hurt us. Things that happen may disappoint us or make us sad. When sufferings like these come, we can pray and ask Jesus to help us accept them as he did. Then he will use these sufferings to bring us closer to him.

Jesus promised that those who suffer with him will be with him in heaven. He will share his glory with those who have shared his cross. We Christians can be happy with Jesus no matter what happens. We know that our sufferings can lead us to eternal happiness with God.

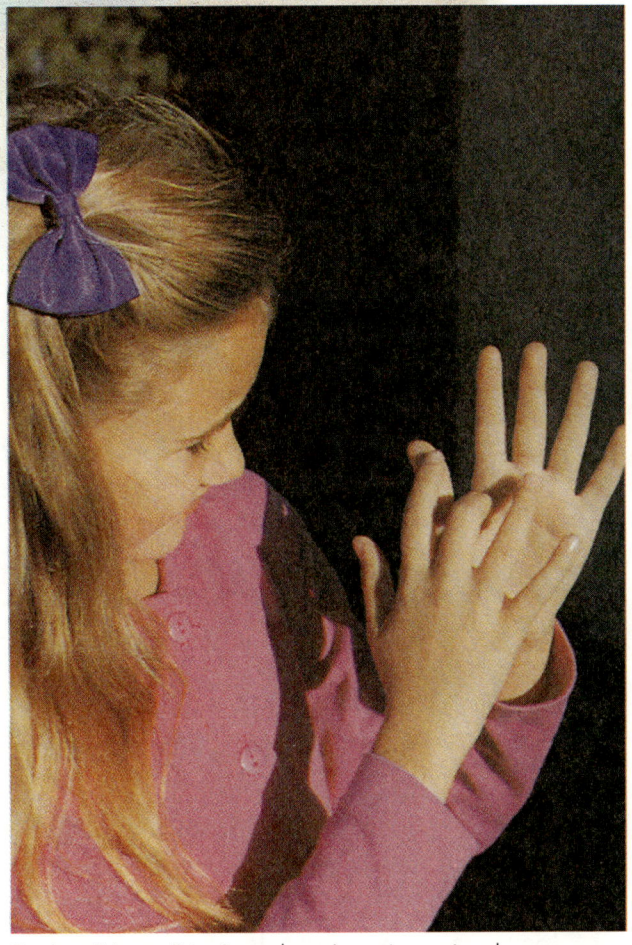

Saying "Jesus" in Ameslan, American sign language

Put These Events in Order

Number these sentences in the order in which they happened. You may look back at the play. Do Set A first and then Set B.

Set A

____ Judas betrayed Jesus with a kiss.
____ The guards made fun of Jesus during the night.
____ The soldiers arrested Jesus in the garden.
____ Jesus was taken to the high priest's house to be questioned.
____ The disciples all ran away.

Set B

____ Jesus was nailed to the cross.
____ The soldiers made a crown of thorns and put it on Jesus' head.
____ Pilate handed Jesus over to the soldiers to be whipped.
____ Jesus died at three o'clock on Friday.
____ Jesus was taken to Pilate.

Across

2. The hill where Jesus was crucified was _____.
3. The governor who gave Jesus over to the soldiers was _____.
4. The sign of Jesus' death is a _____.
7. Jesus celebrated the Jewish feast of _____.
9. By his death Jesus showed his great _____.
10. Jesus prayed to his _____.

Down

1. Jesus' final meal with his apostles was the _____ _____.
5. Jesus still offers himself on our altars at _____.
6. Jesus saved us by his suffering _____.
8. Jesus was disappointed when his apostles couldn't keep awake for an _____.

The Places of the Passion

Find the places where Jesus prayed and suffered. Write the number in the correct circle. Then trace the journey of Jesus with a crayon.

1. Garden where Jesus prayed
2. Home of the Roman governor
3. Place where Jesus was crucified
4. Place where Jesus was questioned
5. Place where the people gathered
6. Place where Jesus ate with his apostles

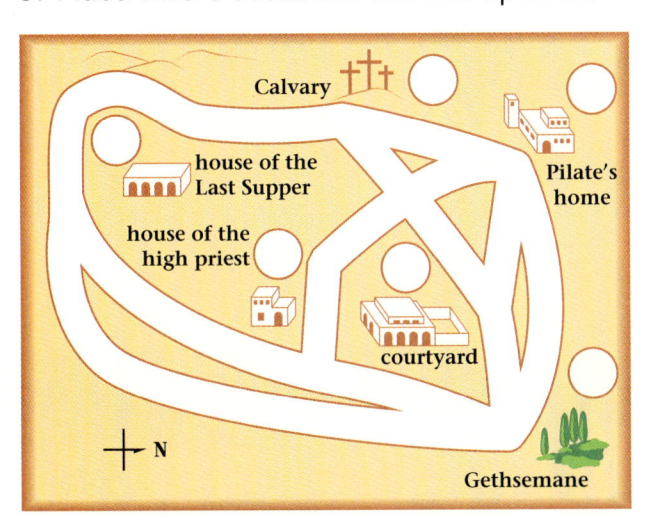

We Remember

What is the sacrifice of the New Covenant?
The sacrifice of the New Covenant is the Mass.

What is the law of the New Covenant?
The law of the New Covenant is "As I have loved you, so also should you love one another."

Why did Jesus willingly accept suffering and death?
Jesus willingly accepted suffering and death to save us from sin and death because he loved the Father and us.

We Respond

We adore you, O Christ, and we praise you, because by your holy cross you have redeemed the world.

FAMILY CORNER

Jesus suffered for our sins because he loved his Father and us. We can unite our suffering with his and pray for strength when in difficulty.

Read
Luke 22:39–46

Discuss
- What did Jesus tell the disciples to pray for when they were in Gethsemane? Why is prayer important?
- How did the Father comfort his Son, Jesus?

Pray
Passion of Christ, strengthen me.

Do
- Share what you think was Jesus' greatest suffering in each Passion event. Find pictures of people suffering like Jesus.
- Help someone who is suffering.
- Pray a decade of the sorrowful mysteries for grace to follow Jesus even in suffering.
- Take part in the Holy Week services.
- Make a table centerpiece having wheat and grapes, symbols of the Eucharist.
- During Holy Week read the Bible before meals (Mk 14:22–25; 14:66–72; Matt 27:27–31; Lk 22:63–65; Jn 19:25–27).

❑ Signature

22 Jesus Is Risen

The Risen Jesus Brings Peace and Joy

Mark an X before each fear you think is real for children your age.

_____ fear they won't have friends

_____ fear someone they love will die

_____ fear of the dark

_____ fear their parents don't love them

_____ fear of dogs

_____ fear someone might make them try drugs or cigarettes

_____ fear of reading out loud

_____ fear older children will beat them up

_____ fear their parents will be divorced

_____ fear they will lose their friends if they disagree with them

_____ fear of a nuclear war

All of us have fears. Jesus wants us to remember that he is always with us. He wants us to trust in his love and care. When we feel afraid, we can say, "Jesus, I trust in your loving care." Then we can forget our fears and let love grow in our hearts.

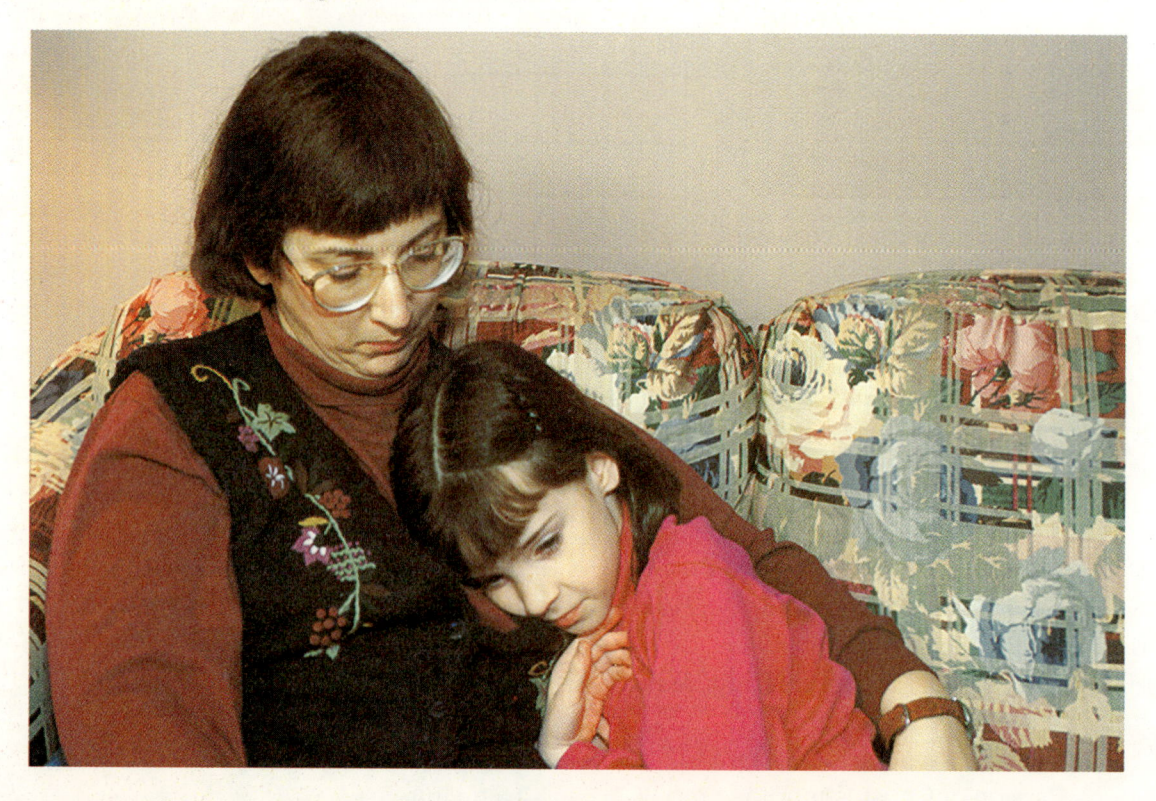

Early on the first day of the week, some women found Jesus' tomb empty. Stories spread quickly. "His body has been stolen!" "He has risen and is alive!" What was the truth?

In the evening the disciples were gathered together behind locked doors. They were afraid of the people who had killed Jesus. Some disciples said that they had seen Jesus. They knew that he had been dead, but now he was alive. It sounded impossible! If he was alive, what did it mean? What did it mean to them?

Suddenly Jesus came and stood among them. He said, "Peace be with you" and showed them his hands and his side. The disciples were filled with joy when they saw the Lord. He said again, "Peace be with you. As the Father has sent me, so I send you."

After saying this, he breathed on them and said: "Receive the holy Spirit. Whose sins you forgive, are forgiven them."

adapted from John 20:19–23

The disciples knew then that Jesus was truly the Lord. He had come now to take away all their fears. They were filled with hope and peace. The disciples would spread the good news that Jesus was risen. He had restored the eternal life of grace that had been lost by sin. Through them he would forgive sins. Then the disciples would bring his peace to people everywhere.

We Work for Peace

The girl in the picture brought messages of peace from Russian children. Everyone who works for peace helps build a better world. Christians are called to go out and bring Jesus' peace to the ends of the earth.

How can you bring Jesus' message of peace to your family and other people you meet?

We Celebrate Easter

Easter, the day we celebrate Jesus' resurrection, is the greatest feast of the whole year. It is Christ's great victory over sin and death. This victory is so great that we celebrate it every Sunday. We have a special eucharistic celebration this first day of the week. It should be a day of joy, relaxation, and peace. This is our response to all Jesus has done for us.

Sunday is a day of celebration for all who follow Jesus.

How are the families in these pictures making Sunday special?

List two things your family likes to do to celebrate Sunday.

1. _____

   _____

2. _____

   _____

Jesus' Death Brought New Life

The beautiful Easter candle that is lighted at the Easter Vigil is called the **paschal candle.** It reminds us that Jesus, the light of the world, is still with us. We share in the light of this candle. It is a sign that we also share in Jesus' victory over sin and death.

Why, then, do people still die? Jesus' victory changed death to life. When we die, we really begin to live. We live a new life in heaven.

Jesus has prepared a place in heaven for each of us. He has promised that if we love him, we will live with him forever and be perfectly happy. We do not fully understand what that means, but we can trust God. God keeps his word.

Jesus revealed something of the heavenly kingdom to John. In the last book of the Bible, John tells us:

> I heard a loud voice saying, "This is God's home with the human race! He will live among them and they will be his people. God will always be with them as their God. He will wipe every tear from their eyes. There shall be no more death or sorrow, crying or pain, for the old order has passed away."
> adapted from Revelation 21:3–4

Death is the door to heaven. We must die in order to live with Jesus in heaven. At the right moment, Jesus will come and take us to our new home. Then we will be perfectly happy with God, who loves us so much!

Death Is a Time of Sadness and Joy

If death is such a wonderful event, why are we sad when someone dies?

We are sad when someone dies because we miss the person we have loved. Jesus was sorrowful when his friend Lazarus died. He went to the place where Lazarus was buried, and he cried. The people knew that Jesus loved Lazarus and missed him. Jesus shows us that it is all right to be sad when someone we love dies.

Death is a time when we can be both happy and sad. We can be happy because, through death, we go home to God. We will know and love God in a new way in heaven. We will see God's goodness and beauty. We will be filled forever with a joy greater than we can ever know on earth. We will never suffer or be sad again.

But for those left behind on earth, there is sadness. It is hard to say good-bye to someone we love. No matter how many people we love, each one is special. No one else can take that person's place.

When someone we love dies, Jesus understands how we feel and wants to comfort us. He also wants us to continue to show love for people who have died. We can pray for them. We can show respect for their bodies by burying them reverently and by visiting their graves.

Find the Mystery Words
Write the missing letters on the blanks.

1. By his resurrection Jesus overcame sin and __ __ __ t __ .

2. The feast on which we celebrate Jesus' resurrection is __ __ s __ __ __ .

3. If we trust Jesus, he can take away our f __ __ __ __ .

4. We celebrate the resurrection of the Lord each __ __ __ __ __ y.

5. When we die, Jesus will take us home to __ __ __ v __ __ .

We Remember

Why do we celebrate Jesus' resurrection?
We celebrate Jesus' resurrection because when he destroyed death he showed he was God and made it possible for us to live with him forever in heaven.

We Respond

I will try to live as a follower of Jesus, our risen Lord. I will say, "Jesus, I trust in your loving care."

Alleluia! The Lord Is Risen

FAMILY CORNER

Through his resurrection Jesus destroyed death, restored the eternal life of grace, and gave us his peace. Death is the door to heaven, but it is a time of mixed emotions.

Read
John 20:19–23

Discuss
- How did Jesus greet his disciples? Why may he have chosen this greeting?
- From what fears did Jesus want to free the apostles?
- What sacrament did Jesus give at Easter? Why was this a perfect Easter gift?

Pray
I long to see your face, O Lord!

Do
- Read the Gospel story about the women finding the empty tomb (Luke 24:1–8). Ponder the meaning of the angel's words.
- Sing an Easter hymn before a meal.
- Have family members complete "One time I was afraid that . . ." Consider how people we love help us conquer fears.
- As a family, visit a cemetery—if possible, the grave of a relative or friend. Share happy memories as well as the sorrow you felt when the person died. Talk about why this is a holy place. Pray there.
- Plan one thing your family can do each Sunday, besides celebrating Mass, to keep the Sabbath holy.

❑ Signature

23 Jesus Christ Is Lord and King

Jesus Returned in Glory to His Father

In the Bible, the last time Jesus appeared to his disciples, he gave them this message:

> "Go, therefore, and make disciples of all nations, baptizing them in the name of the Father, and of the Son, and of the holy Spirit, teaching them to observe all that I have commanded you. And behold, I am with you always, until the end of the age."
>
> Matthew 28:19–20

Jesus also told them to return to Jerusalem and wait for the coming of the Holy Spirit. They would receive power from the Holy Spirit and become Christ's witnesses before the whole world.

After saying these things Jesus raised his hands in blessing. The disciples saw Jesus being lifted up. Then a cloud covered him, and they could see him no more. The Church celebrates this mystery forty days after Easter, on **Ascension Thursday.**

adapted from The Acts of the Apostles 1:4–8, Luke 24:50

May Christ Reign in Our Hearts

The time of a king's rule is called a **reign.** If something happens while a king is ruling, we say that it takes place during the reign of that king. Christ the King will rule, or reign, forever. His reign will never end.

Wherever Christ reigns, there is truth, justice, and peace. Every person is respected and treated fairly. The weak are protected, and the strong work to make life happier for all.

Jesus does not force us to accept him as our king. We can choose to be greedy and selfish. We can choose to say and do things that hurt ourselves and others. But we will be happy only when we live in love. In Christ's kingdom love reigns. We let Christ reign in our hearts when we listen to him and do whatever he says.

> Sing praise to God, sing praise;
> sing praise to our king, sing praise.
> God is king over all the earth;
> sing hymns of praise.
> God rules over the nations;
> God sits upon his holy throne.
> Psalm 47:7–9

During every Mass, we proclaim God as king. At the end of the prayer after the Our Father, we praise God.

For the kingdom, the power and the glory are yours, now and forever.

A Crisscross Puzzle

Read the sentences and complete the puzzle with the correct word.

1. Forty days after Easter Jesus ascended into _____ .
2. Jesus gave a farewell message to his _____ .
3. The Church celebrates Jesus' return to heavenly glory on _____ Thursday.
4. Jesus told his disciples to teach all _____ .
5. Jesus sent his disciples to be his _____ before the whole world.

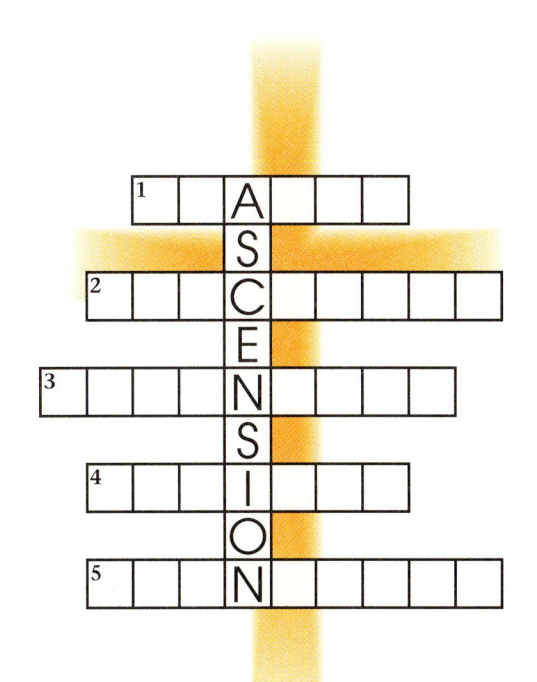

Jesus My King

Find the sentences that tell something you can do to show that Jesus is your king. Print the numbers of these sentences in the jewels on the crown. Then print *Christ the King* in the crown.

1. Say something friendly to a child who looks lonely or sad.
2. Tease little children.
3. Send a card to someone who is lonely or sick.
4. Complain about food and other things you don't like.
5. Be patient when others do something that upsets you.
6. Argue with your brothers and sisters.
7. Refuse to share new things that you really like.
8. Look only at pictures and shows that will help you think and do good things.
9. Pray for other people.
10. Sulk when you don't get what you want.

151

A Picture Study

1. Behind Jesus can be seen the symbol of the _____.

2. Jesus looks like a lord and _____.

3. He is sitting on a _____.

4. The book he has might be the _____.

5. His hand is raised in _____.

Jesus Will Come Again

Jesus will come again in glory at the end of time to judge all people. Jesus told his disciples about this judgment. He said, "The Son of Man will come with all his angels and take his seat on his throne. All the people of the earth will be gathered before him. He will separate them into two groups, as a shepherd separates the sheep and the goats."
adapted from Matthew 25:31–33

The king will say to those on his right hand, "Come, you who are blessed by my Father. Receive the kingdom prepared for you from the creation of the world. For I was hungry and you gave me food. I was thirsty and you gave me drink. I was a stranger and you welcomed me. I was naked and you clothed me. I was sick and you visited me, in prison and you came to see me."

Then these people will say, "Lord, when did we see you in want and do these things for you?"

The king will answer them, "Whenever you did this to one of the least of mine, you did it to me."

Next he will say to those on his left hand, "Go away from me, to the eternal fire prepared for the devil and his angels. For I was hungry and you gave me no food. I was thirsty and you gave me no drink. I was a stranger and you did not make me welcome, naked and you did not clothe me. I was sick and in prison and you did not care for me."

Then they will ask, "When did we see you in want and not take care of your needs?"

The king will answer them. "What you did not do for one of these least ones, you did not do for me."

They will go away to eternal punishment, and the good will go to eternal life.
adapted from Matthew 25:34–46

How Can We Show Mercy to Others?

Read the sentences. Answer the questions.

1. My favorite television program is on at the same time as the special my parents want to watch. What should I do?

2. Lia knows where to get drugs and wants me to try some. Kids say they are great. What should I do?

3. My grandmother who lives with us is upset when my friend and I are noisy. What should I do?

4. The teacher asked for volunteers to make thank-you cards at recess. I am good in art but like to play then. What should I do?

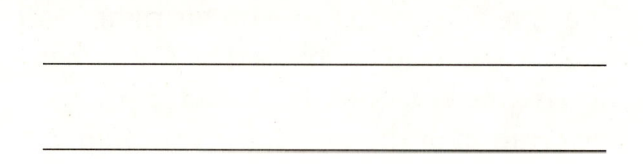

5. Rob is passing around a magazine with bad pictures and wants me to look at it. What should I do?

6. Doris gets all A's on her report card and brags about it. I feel envious. What should I do?

7. I received a new ball and mitt for my birthday. My sister wishes she had one. What should I do?

8. My brothers and sisters left a mess. I know that my mother will not like it. What should I do?

154

Mother Teresa was a witness to Jesus. Her Sisters carry on her work of loving him in the poorest of the poor.

We Remember

How do we know that whatever we do for others we do for Jesus?

Jesus said, "Whatever you do for one of the least of mine, you do for me."
adapted from Matthew 25:40

We Respond

Jesus, I love you.

FAMILY CORNER

Jesus, Lord and King, will come again to judge all people. We show love for him by loving others and being generous in serving him.

Read
Matthew 25:31–46

Discuss
- How will Jesus come to judge all nations?
- What will the King praise the good people for doing?
- Why will he curse the wicked?
- What will be the reward of the good? the punishment of the wicked?

Pray
Praise and honor to you, Lord Jesus Christ.

Do
- Have a blessed candle on the table and light it before dinner. Let it burn during the meal as a sign that Jesus is with you.
- Have the family members name the acts of kindness or mercy on which all people will be judged. Tell how the family and individuals can feed the hungry, give drink to the thirsty, welcome the stranger, clothe the naked, visit the sick, visit the imprisoned, and shelter the homeless.
- When you view television together, look for acts of mercy practiced or neglected. You may wish to find stories in the newspaper that show the same.
- Choose one act of mercy that the family can do this week for Jesus.

❏ Signature

24 Jesus Gives His Spirit to the Church

Jesus Sent the Holy Spirit on Pentecost

Before Jesus died he made a very special promise to his apostles. He told them:

> "I will send you the Helper, the Holy Spirit, who knows all truth. He comes from the Father and will teach you all about me. Then you can teach other people about me because you have been with me from the beginning."
>
> adapted from John 15:26–27

Jesus kept his promise after he returned to heaven. The apostles waited in Jerusalem as Jesus had told them to do. Mary, the mother of Jesus, was with them. While they waited for the Holy Spirit, they prayed. Suddenly, there was the sound of a loud wind. Something like tongues of fire rested on the heads of those who were there. The Holy Spirit had come! Wind and fire are signs of the Spirit. We celebrate this event on **Pentecost.**

Jesus had sent his Spirit to work in and through the apostles. They were the leaders of his Church. The Holy Spirit helped them to grow in love for God and understand what Jesus had taught. He helped them to act more like Jesus. The Holy Spirit made it possible for the apostles to carry on what Jesus had done.

- They did the will of God our Father.
- They did works of love.
- They taught all that Jesus had said.
- They prayed as Jesus had taught them.
- They forgave sins.
- They worked and suffered to spread the kingdom of God.
- They offered Jesus' own sacrifice to the Father.

The Holy Spirit had come with power to help the whole Church do what Jesus had done. The Church is the People of God. We are God's people today. We must listen to the Holy Spirit, obey our Church leaders, and do the work of Jesus.

Make up two prayers for God's people today and write them on the lines. Use the list of things the Holy Spirit helped the apostles to do. One is done for you.

Come, Holy Spirit, _____ help us do works of love as Jesus did. _____

Come, Holy Spirit, _____

_____.

Come, Holy Spirit, _____

_____.

Draw a picture of yourself or friends doing a work of Jesus. Write a title for your picture on the line below it.

The Spirit of Jesus Is with Us

The Holy Spirit came at Baptism to live within our hearts. He gives us the grace to love God and others more. He helps us understand God's great love for us. The Holy Spirit has special gifts for us that help us pray and do the work of Jesus in the world.

The Spirit speaks quietly, often when we aren't expecting him. We don't want to miss his voice, so we must always be ready and listening!

Put the words below in the correct order. Then you will know how to be ready for the gifts of the Holy Spirit. The first word of each sentence is given.

1. Have _____.
quiet time to God talk to some

2. Pray, "_____."
Spirit Come Holy

3. Do _____.
what you asks God

4. Use _____.
grace the Spirit's Holy of gifts

5. Thank _____.
his Spirit for the Holy gifts

Discover the Secrets

You can ask the Holy Spirit to help you discover the secrets about God.

Read these messages carefully and choose one word from each message that reminds you of God. Print each word in a box. Then decorate it.

First Secret Word

The great God who has created all things is our Father! He loves us more than we can imagine. Jesus is happy to share his Father's love with us. He called God "Abba, Father." Jewish children used this name—like Dad—for their earthly fathers. Jesus tells us that we too may call God by that name. How wonderful it is that our great, almighty God is our loving heavenly Father!

Second Secret Word

Jesus, who loved us so much that he suffered and died for us, is the Lord! When Jesus returned to heaven after his resurrection, God the Father made him Lord of heaven and earth! This Jesus, the Lord, wants us to love him and come to him with our joys and sorrows. He wants to be our friend. The Holy Spirit wants us to love Jesus and become like him.

We can use these two special words when we pray to God. The Holy Spirit is with us and will give us the grace to pray and grow in love.

Mary Was Filled with the Spirit

Mary knew God better, and loved God more, than any other person. She was full of grace, and the Holy Spirit was always with her. The Holy Spirit came to Mary, though, in a special way at the Annunciation and on Pentecost and helped her to do loving deeds. Think about these events in Mary's life. Ask Mary to help you know and do all that the Holy Spirit asks!

Write about Mary's loving deeds at these special times.

Mary's relative Elizabeth was expecting a baby.
_____ .

Mary and Jesus were at the wedding at Cana.
_____ .

Jesus was dying on the cross.
_____ .

We Remember

What does the Holy Spirit do for us?
The Holy Spirit helps us to know and love God, pray, and do the work of Jesus.

Word to Know
Pentecost

We Respond

Come, Holy Spirit!

FAMILY CORNER

The Holy Spirit empowers the Church to carry on the work of Jesus, enlightening and strengthening us to do all that God asks.

Read
Acts 2:1–6

Discuss
- What were the signs of the coming of the Holy Spirit to the apostles?
- Why were these good signs for the Holy Spirit?
- Who came to see what happened? What did they find?
- When might you need grace to be strong enough to do what God wants?

Pray
Come, Holy Spirit, show me your way.

Do
- Make name cards for your Sunday dinner table. Draw flames and print *Holy Spirit, come to [Name]*.
- Make a banner for your prayer corner, asking the Holy Spirit to be with you.
- Find pictures of people doing Christ's work. Discuss how each person needs the Holy Spirit and how your patron saints responded to the Holy Spirit.

_____
❏ Signature

25 We Belong to the Kingdom

Jesus Unites Us in the Communion of Saints

All the people who belong to Christ the King are joined to God and to one another by his love. We call this union the **communion of saints.** Everyone in the communion of saints works together to praise God and to bring Christ's love to all.

All baptized people belong to the communion of saints.

Write here the names of people you love who are members of the communion of saints on earth.

_____

_____

_____

_____

People in purgatory belong to the communion of saints.

These people did believe in Jesus, but they were not perfect in love. These holy souls suffer to make up for their sins and because they long to be with God in heaven. They are happy too. They know that they will be with God when they are free from selfishness, sin, and sin's effects.

Write here the names of some members of the communion of saints who have died.

_____

_____

_____

_____

The thousands of saints who are in heaven belong to the communion of saints.

The saints pray for us and ask God to give us grace and blessings. Their lives can teach us how to become holy. All of us have patron saints in heaven who watch over us with special love. Maybe some of our relatives and friends are now saints in heaven.

Write here the names of some of your favorite saints.

_____

_____

_____

The members of the communion of saints are all one in Christ. Just as in any family, each member helps the others. The saints in heaven, the souls in purgatory, and the baptized people on earth help us to be faithful to God by their prayers. We pray and do good for all the members of the communion of saints on earth. We help the people in purgatory by our prayers and good works.

One In Christ

Find the word in the gift box that completes each sentence. Write the words on the lines.

1. People on earth who believe in Jesus and are baptized belong to the communion of _____ .

2. All in the communion of saints are united in Christ's _____ .

3. Those who believed in Jesus but died before their love was perfect are purified in _____ .

4. We call the people in purgatory the _____ .

5. Members of the communion of saints who are perfectly happy are in _____ .

heaven
saints
purgatory
love
holy souls

Mary Is Queen of Heaven and Earth
At the end of Mary's life on earth, she was taken body and soul into heavenly glory. Mary shared in the resurrection of Jesus. We call this the **Assumption.** In heaven she now rejoices with the angels and saints. We celebrate the Assumption on August 15.

God made Mary the queen of heaven and earth. God wants Mary to take care of us. She helps us to follow Jesus. This is why we pray to her. Someday, through death, we can share with Jesus in the glory of the Resurrection. Our bodies will be glorified, too. We will be united with Jesus, Mary, the angels, the saints, and all those we love in heaven.

What prayer can we pray to Mary to ask her to help us love God?

A Song to Mary, Queen of Heaven and Earth

Hail, Holy Queen, Enthroned Above

1. Hail, Holy Queen, enthroned above,
   O Maria!
   Hail, Mother of Mercy and of Love,
   O Maria!

   Refrain:
   Triumph, all ye cherubim.
   Sing with us, ye seraphim.
   Heav'n and earth resound the hymn:
   Salve, salve, salve Regina!

2. And when our life on earth is done,
   O Maria,
   Then show us Christ, thy holy Son,
   O Maria!

From the Litany of Our Lady

Response: *Pray for us.*
  Holy Mary,
  Holy Mother of God,
  Mother of Christ,
  Mother most pure,
  Mother most
    merciful,
  Virgin most faithful,
  Help of Christians,
  Queen of apostles
    and martyrs,
  Queen of all saints,
  Queen of the most
    holy rosary,
  Queen of peace.

Let us pray:

  O God, give us
    health. Through
  Mary's prayers for us,
  free us from sin and
  bring us to eternal
  happiness through
  Christ our Lord.
            Amen.

We Honor Mary

Our Lady of the Rockies is a ninety-foot-high statue in Montana. The Church honors Mary because she is the mother of Jesus. When we honor Mary, we praise God because God gave her the gifts of holiness and faithfulness.

We honor Mary by many titles in the Litany of Our Lady. As we say each title, we think of a special gift God gave her. After we say each title, we ask Mary to pray for us. She will ask Jesus for the grace we need to be holy.

Acting like a Member of the Communion of Saints
Write under each picture what you can do to be a faithful person like Mary.

167

Choosing Fun
Underline the best choice to complete each sentence.

1. Jesus said he came into the world to (save, condemn, reject) the world.

2. Jesus said that we do for him what we (do in church, say in our prayers, do for others).

3. Jesus said his followers must (carry their cross, work for more money, seek a good job).

4. People who must make up for sins after death are in (heaven, purgatory, hell).

5. The sacrifice of the New Covenant is the (Sacrament of Reconciliation, Mass celebration, Passover celebration).

6. The Holy Spirit came to (guide, judge, punish).

7. Jesus will share his glory with those who are (smart, loving, rich).

Lord   reigns
Communion
judge   happiness
glory   King

Acrostic
Fill in the missing letters. Use the words in the crown.

Jesus is our K __ __ __ .

He __ __ i __ __ __ in heaven and on earth.

Jesus promised __ __ __ __ __ n __ __ __ to us.

He invites us to share his g __ __ __ __ .

Jesus will come to __ __ d __ __ all people at the end of time.

He will be __ o __ __ forever and ever.

We are one with him in __ __ m __ __ __ __ __ already.

We Belong to God's Kingdom
Print the correct letters on the lines.

1. Jesus is truly the S __ __ of God.

2. Jesus r __ __ __ from the dead.

3. Jesus returned to his Father in g __ __ __ __ .

4. Our bodies will r __ __ __ on the last day as Jesus promised.

5. All those who die to s __ __ will share in the glory of the risen Jesus.

6. The s __ __ __ __ __ in heaven pray to God for us.

7. The Holy S __ __ __ __ __ gives us grace to be strong Christians.

We Remember

What is the communion of saints?
The communion of saints is the union of all those who belong to Christ the King. It includes all the saints in heaven, the souls in purgatory, and baptized people on earth.

Why do we honor Mary?
We honor Mary because she is the mother of Jesus. We praise God for her many gifts.

Word to Know
Assumption

We Respond

Holy Mary, Mother of God,
pray for us sinners,
now and at the hour
of our death.

FAMILY CORNER

The communion of saints is the union of all people in heaven, on earth, and in purgatory who believe and follow Jesus. We on earth have daily opportunities to acknowledge Christ as King of our hearts.

Read
John 14:1–4

Discuss
- Why doesn't Jesus want us to worry?
- What will he prepare for us in heaven?

Pray
Lord, I believe in you!

Do
- Let each family member read about the life of a saint. Share what you like about him or her.
- Comment on how the actions of world leaders promote justice or injustice.
- On a family walk note new life and growth resulting from spring. Compare it with the new life of heaven.
- Invite the family of your child's classmate to your home. Share the activities you have done. End with prayer and refreshments.

❏ Signature

We Look Back over the Year

Work the puzzle, using the words around it.

Across

2. We hope to reach heaven because we _____ in God.
4. Our belief in God is called _____ .
6. Jesus came to save. He is our _____ .
8. By his words and deeds God _____ himself.
10. God has pity on us. God is _____ .
12. God wants us to do good _____ .
13. Jesus reigns as _____ of heaven and earth.
15. Our sharing in God's life is called _____ .

Down

1. To follow Jesus we must be brave and have _____ .
3. Jesus died and _____ to save us.
4. When we are sorry for sin, God is _____ .
5. Jesus, you _____ Lord.
7. We praise God when we say _____ .
9. Jesus is _____ of all.
11. On Easter Sunday night Jesus gave us his _____ .
14. The first woman God made was _____ .

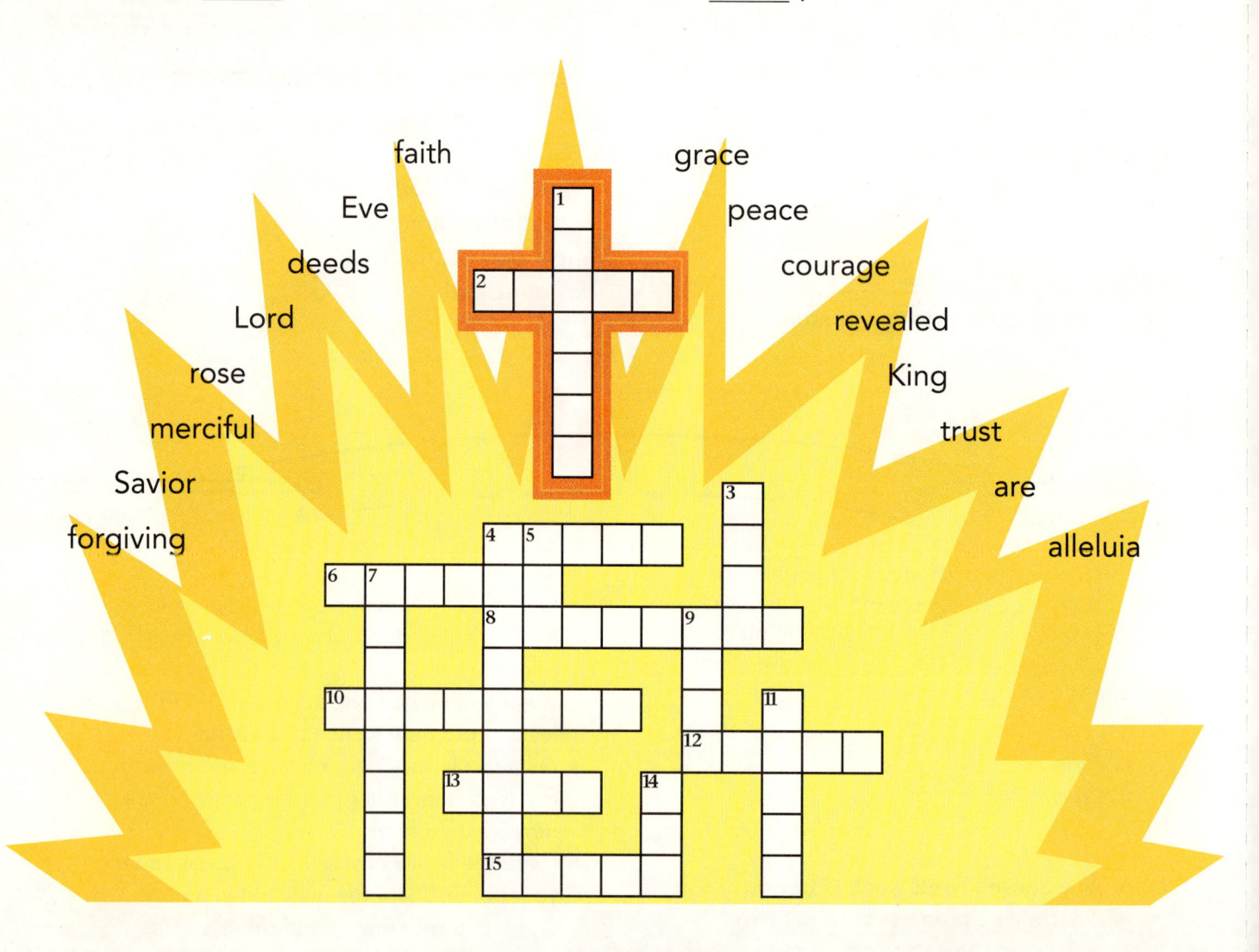

faith
Eve
deeds
Lord
rose
merciful
Savior
forgiving

grace
peace
courage
revealed
King
trust
are
alleluia

Looking Ahead

Plan to spread Jesus' kingdom during your summer vacation.

Finish each sentence by telling when, how, or for whom you will do these things.

I will take part in Mass _____.

I will receive Holy Communion _____.

I will celebrate the Sacrament of Reconciliation _____.

I will show respect for _____ and _____.

I will obey _____.

I will pray _____.

I will help _____.

Save your book, *We Believe,* to read from at least once a week.
Use a bookmark. Enjoy reading over what it means to be a Catholic Christian.

Come, Lord Jesus

Song and Procession

Readings

Reader 1: We are never alone on our journey of faith to heaven. We are part of a great family of saints. The whole family of God in heaven, in purgatory, and on earth is united in God's life and his love. This union of God's children, the communion of saints, will last forever in heaven.

Reader 2: We are waiting for the coming of Jesus and the kingdom of heaven. We wait in joy, looking forward to all the wonderful things God has promised to those who are faithful. While we wait, we pray, love, and serve. We try to do all the good we can. We try to spread God's kingdom—to bring his truth and love to others. This is how Jesus wants us to wait for his coming.

Reader 3: See that you are prepared; have your lamps lit. Be like servants waiting for their master to return, ready to open the door as soon as he comes and knocks. How happy will those servants be whom the master finds ready when he comes!

adapted from Luke 12:35–37

Leader: We will light candles as a sign that we want to be ready when God calls us to heaven.

(Light candles.)

Reader 4: The burning lamp is a symbol of our faith. We keep our lamps burning by living in faith, hope, and love until Jesus comes to call us home forever. St. John wrote in the last book of the Bible about waiting for the Lord's return. Jesus revealed this message to John for his Church.

Reader 5: I am coming soon! Let those who do good keep on doing good. Those who are holy must keep on being holy. I am coming soon! I will bring with me the reward for everyone according to what he or she deserves. Yes, I am coming soon!

adapted from Revelation 22:11–12, 20

Reader 6: In response to this message, St. John wrote the closing words of Sacred Scripture:

All: Amen! Come, Lord Jesus!

(Put out candles.)

Prayers

Leader: Let us pray to our patron saints. Each of us may name his or her own saint, and all of us will answer, "Pray for us." We may also include names of people we have known who are now in eternity.

(Prayers may be said or sung.)

1. Saint Ann, pray for us!
2. Saint Joseph, pray for us!
3. Saint Anthony, pray for us!

All: Dear saints of God, you followed Jesus faithfully on earth and now enjoy the reward Jesus promised. Pray for us who still struggle against sin. Obtain for us the help we need to serve God faithfully. May we one day be with you in the heavenly kingdom. Amen.

Family Activities for the Summer

FAMILY CORNER

These activities will help the children to learn, from the example set by the families and the rest of the Christian community, how to grow in living their faith and use some of their leisure time in order to strengthen their relationship with God and others in their families and the community.

Read
Sunday Gospels
If your parish does not list references for Sunday Scripture readings in its bulletin, copy the Gospel reference from the missalette to read from your Bible or missal.

Discuss
- Who is with Jesus in today's Gospel?
- What is Jesus doing—teaching? healing? praying? something else?
- What message has Jesus for us this week?
- How can we respond to his message?

Pray
Praise and thank God through all your summer activities by praying often "All for you, most Sacred Heart of Jesus."

Do
- Plan to spend some special time together as a family each week. Include fun times, sharing times, and prayer times.
- Look at the stars. Learn the names of some constellations. Stand in awe before God our Creator, who is also our Father.
- June 21 is the longest day of the year. To thank God for the long days of summer fun, visit your parish church as a family. Spend some time there praying quietly, privately and together.
- During July celebrate as a family the Sacrament of Reconciliation. (Help your child prepare by using the leaflet distributed during the study of this sacrament.) Afterward do something your family enjoys.
- August 15 is a holy day of obligation, the Feast of Mary's Assumption. Place flowers before a picture or statue of Mary in your home. Participate in Mass in a parish dedicated to Mary, if possible.
- On your calendar note the first Fridays of the summer months. Show your love for Jesus by receiving Holy Communion as a family on these days.
- Use one of the psalms, such as Psalm 15 or 100, to praise God at mealtime.

❏ Signature

FAMILY FEATURE

Our Ancestors

Jewish people leave a stone on a tombstone each time they visit a grave.

In the Communion of Saints we are still united with those who have gone before us and are now in the next world. In many Latin American countries and in the Philippines, All Souls' Day, or the Day of the Dead, is a feast day and a public holiday. In Mexico on this day the Bartolo family goes to the cemetery dressed in their best clothes. They light candles and kneel at the graves of their departed family members. Mrs. Bartolo decorates the graves with flowers. The family brings food to eat a meal in the presence of their loved ones again.

In the Philippines candles are burned at graves for nine days in preparation for the feast. Graves are trimmed and weeded, and the tombstones cleaned and painted. On the evening of All Souls', young people go from door to door impersonating the holy souls freed from Purgatory and on their way to heaven. They ask for gifts of candy, cookies, and other pastries.

Your family might choose a day such as Memorial Day to recall family members who are no longer on earth. Talk about them, share stories about them, and look through family albums. Offer a Mass and prayers for your departed loved ones. Set their pictures in a place of honor for the day and think of them. Go to the cemetery, clear off their graves, and put flowers by them as a sign that you remember and thank the Lord for those people who have died. Recall something good about each person whose grave you visit and then say a prayer for them.

Christ Saves!

Each Eucharist is a memorial and celebration of Christ's saving acts. We show this in the Eucharistic Prayer when we proclaim the mystery of our faith. Circle the first letter and every other letter below to see what we say.

C P H U R X I W S O T N H Q A M S L

D S I Y E V D X C A H M R Z I E S R

T P I N S C R W I D S G E K N S C L

H U R O I V S N T P W R I B L Y L T

C X O P M L E R A W G S A B I P N !

Friends in the Next World

At the liturgy Mary, the angels, the saints, and holy souls are present with us. In the chalice write the names of people in the next life whom you would like to remember at the next Mass you celebrate.

(Answers: Christ has died, Christ is risen, Christ will come again!)

Easter

Color the jelly beans the colors according to the Easter clues given. Before you color, check your answers.

1. The color of sin and death.
2. The royal color of a king.
3. The color of a sacrifice.
4. The color of hope and life.
5. The color of pure glory.
6. The color of the rising sun.
7. The color of joy.

(Answers: 1. black, 2. purple, 3. red, 4. green, 5. white, 6. yellow, 7. pink)

THE LANDS OF THE OLD TESTAMENT

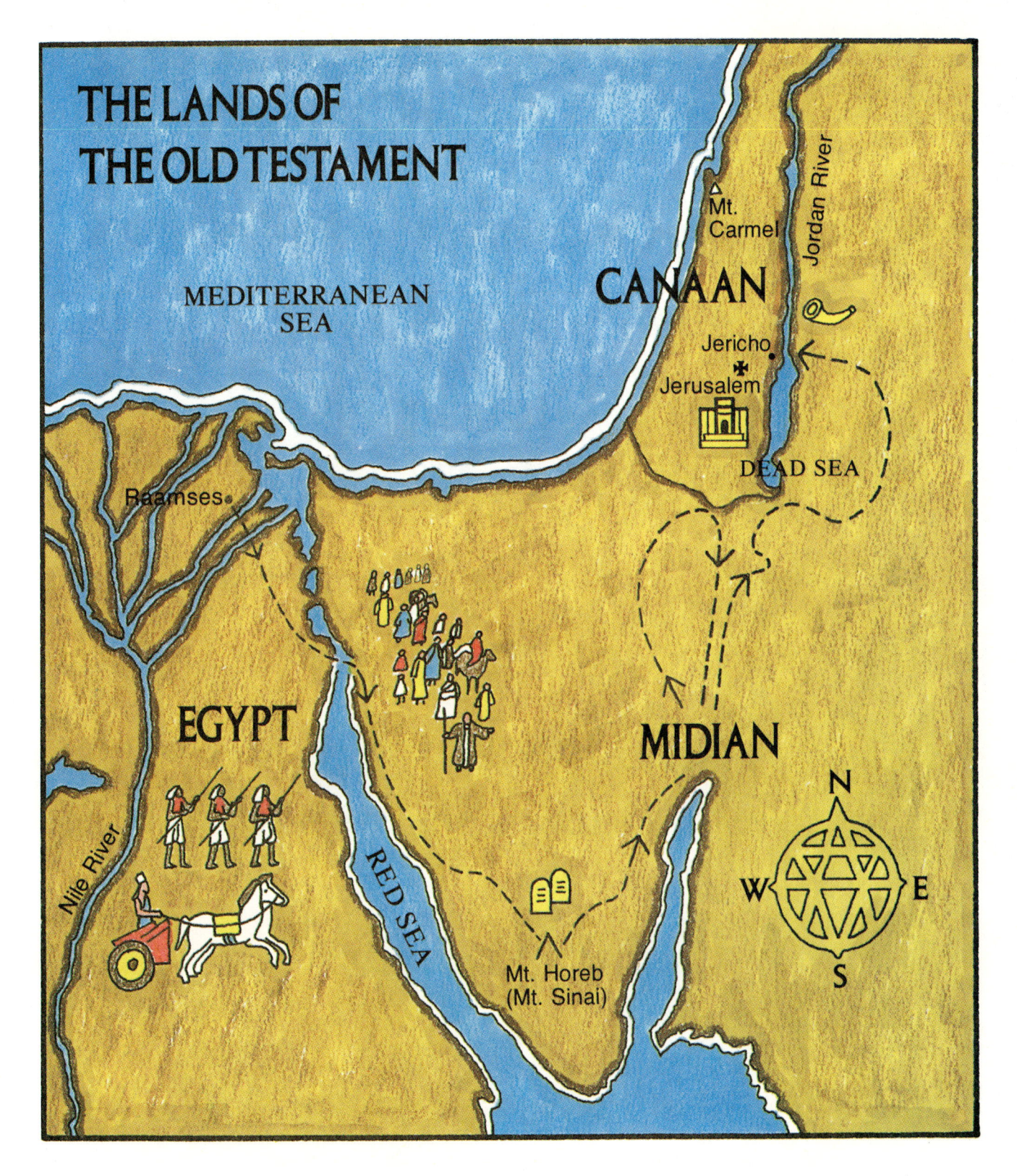

The Old Testament of the Bible tells the story of how God freed his people from slavery in Egypt, led them through the Red Sea, and brought them into the desert. At Mt. Sinai, God gave them his commandments and made a covenant with them. Later he led them into the promised land of Canaan.

PALESTINE IN THE TIME OF JESUS

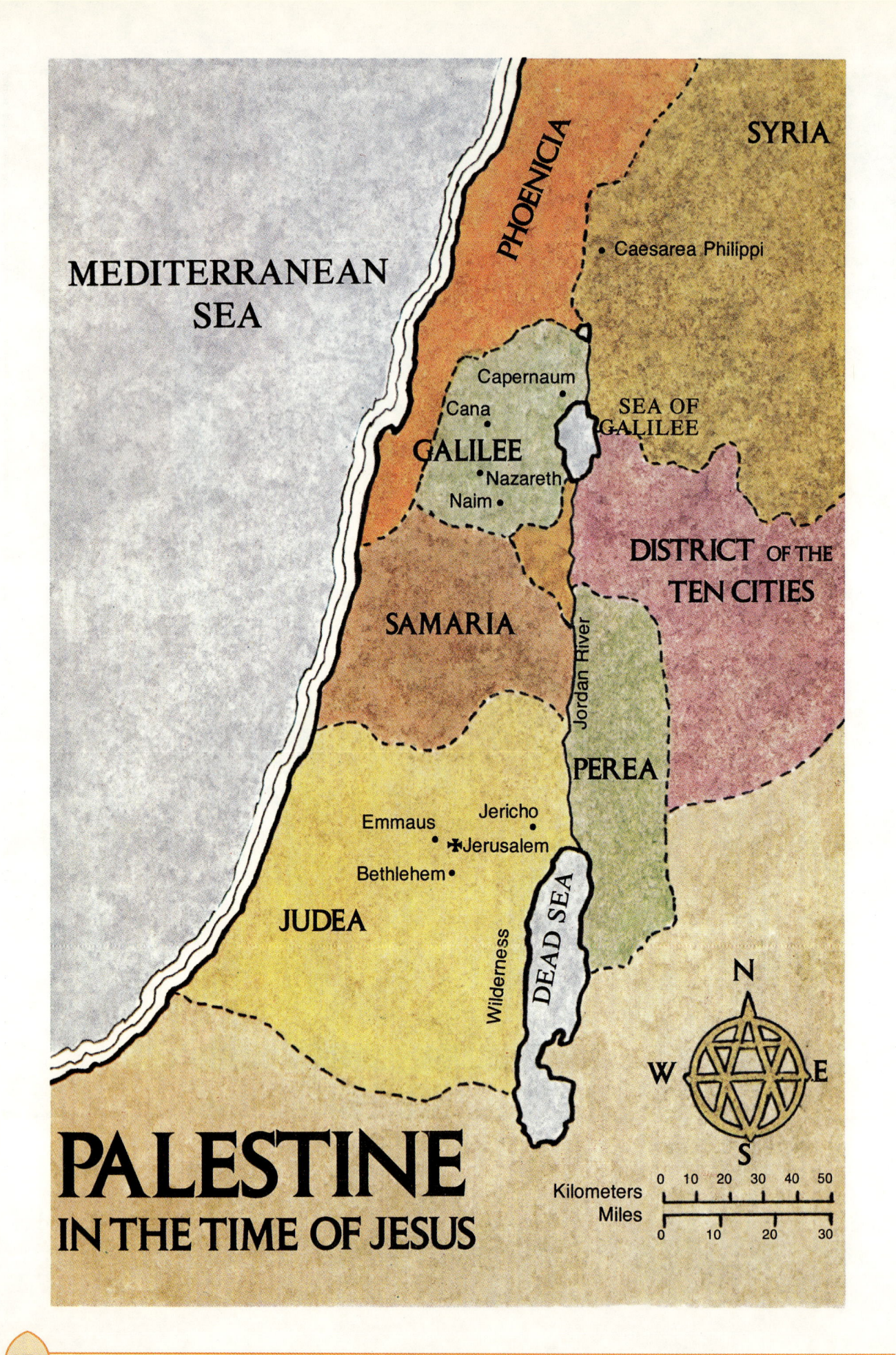

GLOSSARY

Pronunciation Key

a	h*a*llow	ie	l*ie*, sk*y*	uh	r*u*t, *A*scension, hom*i*ly	kw	q*u*it, q*u*arrel
ah	f*a*ther	o	l*o*t	oo	s*oo*n, allel*u*ia	s	*s*tart, pre*ss*, *c*ent
aw	str*aw*, bef*o*re	oh	*o*wn, l*oa*n, l*o*ne	yoo	m*u*sic, b*eau*ty	sh	A*s*cension, sta*ti*on
ay	m*ay*, tr*a*de	ow	c*ow*, h*ou*se	g	*g*et	th	*th*is, for*th*
e	p*e*t, f*ai*r, f*e*rret	oy	b*oy*, b*oi*l	j	*j*uice, e*dge*	z	*z*oo, i*s*
ee	s*ee*n, sc*e*ne	u	f*u*ll, g*oo*d	k	*k*itten, *c*at	zh	mea*s*ure, vi*s*ion
i	h*i*t						

A

absolution (ab suh LOO shuhn): The forgiveness of sins, spoken by the priest in the Sacrament of Reconciliation. The priest gives us *absolution* after we pray an act of contrition.

absolve (uhb ZOLV): 1. To forgive or pardon. 2. To free from sin. Priests receive from Jesus the authority to *absolve* us from our sins.

Advent (AD vent): Four weeks of prayer in preparation for Christmas. During *Advent* Christians do special acts of love.

angel (AYN juhl): A pure, created spirit sent as a messenger from God. An *angel* told Mary she had been chosen to be the Mother of Jesus.

Annunciation (uh nuhn see AY shuhn): The announcement of the Incarnation made by the angel Gabriel to the Virgin Mary. The *Annunciation* of the Lord is celebrated on March 25.

apostle (uh POS uhl): One of the men specially chosen by Jesus to spread his message. An *apostle* carried on the work of Jesus.

Ascension (uh SEN chuhn): The rising of Jesus to heaven on the fortieth day after his resurrection. *Ascension* Thursday is a holy day of obligation in the United States.

Assumption (uh SUHM[P] shuhn): God's bringing Mary to heaven body and soul at the end of her life on earth. The feast of the *Assumption* is celebrated on August 15.

B

Baptism (BAP tiz uhm): The sacrament in which we join in Jesus' death and rising to become children of God and members of the Church, and are cleansed from original sin and our sins. In *Baptism* we receive God's life through water and the words that are said.

Benediction (ben uh DIK shuhn): A prayer service in which we honor Jesus in the Blessed Sacrament and receive his blessing. In *Benediction* the Sacred Host can be seen.

blessed (BLES uhd): Any person, place, or thing specially related to God. It is more *blessed* to give than to receive.

blessing (BLES ing): A prayer asking God to make someone or something holy. The priest gives us a *blessing* at the end of Mass.

C

Church (CHUHRCH): All those who believe in Jesus and are baptized and who follow his teachings. Members of the *Church* are united by their love for Jesus.

communion (kuh MYOO nyuhn) **of saints** (SAYNTS): The union of the saints in heaven, the souls in purgatory, and the Church on earth. Members of the *communion of saints* help one another through their prayers and good works.

conscience (KON shuhns): The judgment of what is the right or wrong thing to do. A Christian should obey his or her *conscience*.

contrition (kuhn TRISH uhn): Sorrow for sin. When we have *contrition,* God forgives us.

177

covenant (KUHV uh nuhnt): An agreement between God and his people. The Hebrew Scriptures describe the *covenant* that God made with the Israelites.

creed (KREED): A summary of the chief truths that we believe. A *creed* tells what we believe.

D

decade (DEK ayd): Set of ten beads in a rosary. We pray ten Hail Marys in a *decade*.

devil (DEV uhl): An evil spirit, especially Satan. The *devil* tempted Jesus in the desert.

disciple (di SIE puhl): A follower of Jesus. A *disciple* of Jesus tries to love others as Christ loves them.

E

eternal (ee TUHRN uhl): Everlasting or endless. Jesus offers us *eternal* life with God in heaven.

Eucharist (YOO k[uh-]ruhst): The sacrament in which Jesus offers himself to his Father for us and then gives us himself in Communion. The *Eucharist* is the Church's greatest prayer and the center of its life.

F

faith (FAYTH): A gift from God that helps us to believe in God and in all he teaches and to trust in his loving care. People of *faith* try to live as God asks them to live.

G

Gospel (GOS puhl): 1. The Good News about Jesus' saving us from sin. 2. Each of the first four books of the New Testament (Matthew, Mark, Luke, and John). The *Gospel* tells us about the life of Jesus Christ and his teachings.

grace (GRAYS): A share in the life of God. Jesus offers us *grace* chiefly through prayer and the sacraments.

H

heaven (HEV uhn): The place where God is with the angels and saints, all those who have loved like Jesus. Jesus made it possible for us to be happy forever in *heaven*.

holy (HOH lee) **souls** (SOHLZ): The souls in purgatory who must make up for sins before they can enter heaven. We pray for the *holy souls* during Mass.

Holy Spirit (SPIR uht): The Third Person of the Trinity, who lives within us and helps us carry on the work of Jesus. We celebrate the coming of the *Holy Spirit* to the Church on Pentecost.

homily (HOM uh lee): The talk that the priest or deacon gives at Mass to explain the readings and how to live them. We are to listen to the *homily* and carry out God's Word.

I

idol (IE duhl): An image of a false god. The pagans often worshiped an *idol* instead of God.

Incarnation (in kar NAY shuhn): The Son of God becoming man. The *Incarnation* is one of the chief mysteries of our faith.

Israelites (IZ r[ee-]uh liets): The name by which the children of Abraham became known; God's chosen people. God delivered the *Israelites* from slavery in Egypt.

J

justice (JUHS tuhs): Giving everyone what he or she deserves; fair treatment. God will show *justice* toward all people.

K

kingdom (KING duhm) **of God:** The reign of God over the hearts and minds of people. We pray that the *kingdom of God* will come to all people.

L

lectionary (LEK shuhn er ee): The book containing the Scripture readings used for the celebration of Mass. The deacon reads the Gospel from the *lectionary*.

Lent: The season of prayer and penance before Easter. *Lent* begins on Ash Wednesday and continues for forty days, until Holy Thursday evening.

Liturgy (LIT uhr jee) **of the Eucharist** (YOO k[uh-]ruhst): The part of the Mass in which Jesus offers himself to the Father for us and gives himself to us in Holy Communion. The *Liturgy of the Eucharist* is the second main part of the Mass.

Liturgy of the Word (WUHRD): The part of the Mass in which we celebrate God's speaking to us. The *Liturgy of the Word* is the first main part of the Mass.

178

M

manna (MAN uh): Special food that God gave the Israelites during their journey in the desert. *Manna* is "the bread from heaven."

mercy (MUHR see): 1. A willingness to help anyone in need. 2. Forgiveness. God's *mercy* is great.

Messiah (mes SIE uh): The Hebrew word for Christ, the Savior who would free the people of Israel. The people in the Old Testament longed for the coming of the *Messiah*.

miracle (MIR i kuhl): A special sign of power Jesus worked to reveal the kingdom of God and to show he had come from God. Jesus' cure of a leper was a *miracle*.

mystery (MIS t[uh-]ree): 1. A truth revealed by God that we cannot completely understand. 2. An event in the life of Jesus, Mary, or the Church that we think about during a decade of the rosary. The truth that God's Son became man is the *mystery* of the Incarnation.

N

New (N[Y]OO) **Covenant** (KUHV uh nuhnt): God's promise to give us eternal life through Jesus if we live as his children. In the *New Covenant* Jesus showed the greatest love and commanded us to love one another as he has loved us.

O

Old (OHLD) **Testament** (TEST uh muhnt): The books of the Bible that tell what God wanted us to know about his plan of salvation before the coming of Christ. The *Old Testament*, sometimes called the Hebrew Scriptures, tells about God's covenant with the Israelites.

original (uh RIJ uh nuhl) **sin:** Our loss of the life of grace because of Adam and Eve's sin. We are born with *original sin*.

P

parable (PAR uh buhl): A short story that teaches a religious truth. A *parable* compares something about the kingdom to ordinary objects or events.

Paschal (PAS kuhl) **Mystery** (MIS t[uh-]ree): The suffering, death, resurrection, and ascension of Jesus. We celebrate the *Paschal Mystery* at every sacrifice of the Mass.

Passover (PAS oh vuhr): The feast the Israelites celebrated to remember that God saved them from slavery in Egypt. Jesus instituted the Eucharist at a *Passover* meal.

Pentecost (PENT i kawst): The fiftieth day after Easter, when the Holy Spirit descended on the apostles. *Pentecost* is the birthday of the Church.

profession (pruh FESH un): A public acceptance of the teachings of the Church. Catholics make a *profession* of faith at Sunday Mass when they say the Creed.

prophet (PROF uht): A person called by God to speak to the people for him. John the Baptist was a great *prophet*.

psalm (SAH[L]M): A prayer-song taken from the Book of Psalms in the Old Testament. A *psalm* is read at Mass.

purgatory (PUHR guh tohr ee): The state after death in which holy souls are made free from the effects of sin before entering heaven. We pray for the souls in *purgatory*.

R

Reconciliation (rek uhn sil ee AY shuhn): The sacrament in which God forgives us our sins if we are sorry. In the Sacrament of *Reconciliation* the priest says words of absolution and we are forgiven.

Redeemer (ri DEE muhr): A title given to Jesus Christ because he made up for our sins. Jesus Christ is our *Redeemer*.

resurrection (rez uh REK shuhn): The rising of Christ from the dead. Every Sunday we celebrate the *resurrection* of Christ.

reveal (ri VEEL): To make known something that is secret or hidden. God is willing to *reveal* himself to us because he loves us.

revelation (rev uh LAY shuhn): God's making himself and his plans known to us. God's *revelation* is found in the Bible and in the teachings of the Church.

rosary (ROHZ [uh] ree): Prayer in which we pray Hail Marys, Our Fathers, and Glory Bes on beads, while we think about the mysteries. There are five decades in the *rosary*.

S

sacrament (SAK ruh muhnt): Special signs that celebrate Jesus' action in our lives. Through each *sacrament* we grow in grace.

sacramental (sak ruh MENT uhl): Words, actions, or things that bring us closer to God. A rosary is a *sacramental*.

sacrifice (SAK ruh fies): A gift offered to God in worship. Jesus' *sacrifice* of himself to God was the one perfect sacrifice.

Sacrifice of the Mass: Jesus' making the offering of himself on the cross present under signs of bread and wine to adore and thank the Father and so to make up for our sins. We participate in the *Sacrifice of the Mass* by praying and singing in union with the priest and others present.

Satan (SAYT uhn): Leader of the evil spirits. His name means "enemy." God allows *Satan* to tempt us.

Savior (SAYV yuhr): A title given to Jesus Christ because he saved us from sin and death. Jesus is Lord and *Savior*.

Scripture (SKRIP chuhr): The Bible. The books of the Old and the New Testaments. *Scripture* is read daily at Mass.

sin: An offense against God; failing to love. We commit a *sin* when we willingly do what we know is wrong.

supernatural (soo puhr NACH [uh] ruhl): Above or beyond what is natural. God gives us *supernatural* life through Baptism.

synagogue (SIN uh gog): A place or building where Jewish people gather for divine worship. Jesus spoke to the people in the *synagogue*.

T

temptation (tem[p] TAY shuhn): Anything that tries to lead us to choose what we know is wrong. A *temptation* is not a sin.

truth (TROOTH): The way things really are. Jesus gave his apostles the power to teach the *truth* about him.

W

witness (WIT nuhss): One who tells what he or she has seen or heard. The apostle Peter was a *witness* of Jesus.

worship (WUHR shuhp): To adore God by prayer and service. We *worship* God at the Sacrifice of the Mass.

Y

Yahweh (YAH way): The name God used to identify himself to Moses. The meaning of the name is "I am who am." *Yahweh* is our God.

INDEX

A

Abraham (Abram), 4–6, 8, 11, 28, 67, 90, 102
Absolution, 48
Act of Contrition, 41, 44–48
Acts of mercy, 154–55
Adam, 30, 97–101, 129
Agony in the Garden, 136
Ahab, 84
Altar, 74, 84–85
Angels, 60, 102–4, 153, 165
Annunciation, 18, 20, 21, 102, 108, 161
Anointing, 11, 13
Apostles, 22, 27, 28, 40, 51, 135–37, 149, 156, 161, 166
Ascension, 20, 149, 151
Assumption, 20, 133, 165, 174

B

Baal, 84–85
Baptism. *See* Sacraments
Belief in God, 3, 5, 8, 31
Benediction, 53
Bethlehem, 7, 11, 103
Bible, 15, 33, 55, 65, 68, 75, 79, 90, 98, 141, 149
Blessed Trinity, 64, 66, 70
Blood of Christ, 51, 74, 94, 135
Body of Christ, 51, 60, 74, 94, 135
Bread, 51, 58, 60, 62, 73, 74, 90, 94, 135

C

Calvary, 138, 140, 141
Canaan, 67, 68, 73, 90
Candle, 107, 146, 155, 172
Catholics, 3, 8, 28, 51, 52, 64, 65
Christian life, 23, 34, 44, 85
    as doing God's will, 106, 117, 157, 158
    as following of Jesus, 95, 106, 117, 144, 157–59
    as sharing the divine life, 44, 96, 97, 101, 115, 117, 159
Christian name, 2, 8
Christians, 3, 6, 8, 23, 27, 32, 65, 117, 139, 144, 169, 171
Christmas, 102, 108, 116
Church, 23, 64, 65, 115, 118, 149
    as family of God, 3, 8, 28, 32, 60, 119, 157, 172
    guided by the Holy Spirit, 15, 81, 133, 161
    leaders in, 15, 22, 157
    presence of Jesus in, 14, 51, 60, 81
Clare, St., 116
Commandments, 33, 35, 44, 70, 75, 77, 84, 87, 89
    fourth, 107, 108
    new, 135
    second, 79, 86
Communion, Holy, 33, 39, 52, 53, 58, 60, 62, 65, 74, 113, 168, 171, 174. *See also* Sacraments, Eucharist
Communion of Saints, 162–64, 167, 169, 172
Confession. *See* Sacraments, Reconciliation
Conscience, 44, 47, 49
Contrition, 40–50
Covenant, 63, 75–77, 87, 91, 102, 135. *See also* New Covenant
Creation, 14, 16, 17, 57
    as means of revealing God, 66, 82, 129, 174
    story of, and the Fall, 100–101
Creed, 64, 70. *See also* Prayers, Apostles' Creed
Crowning with Thorns, 137, 140

D

David, 7, 11–13, 28, 102, 103
Deacons, 23, 27, 56, 61
Death, 68, 146–48
Devil, 98, 153. *See also* Satan
Disappointments, 122
Disciples, 23–28, 44, 143, 144, 148, 149, 151
Duties of Catholic Christians
    to lead a sacramental life, 29, 33, 34, 39, 41, 44, 52, 135
    to observe Sundays and holy days, 44, 51, 56, 62
    to strengthen and support the Church in her mission, 52, 61, 64, 112, 115, 118, 128, 157, 158

E

Easter, 145, 146, 148, 170
Egypt, 67, 68, 102, 135
Elijah, 84–85
Elizabeth, 161
Eternal life, 1, 17, 35, 69, 70, 76, 95, 108, 125, 139, 146, 148, 153
Eucharist. *See* Sacraments
Eve, 30, 97–101, 129, 170
Evil, 30, 98, 114
Examination of conscience, 44, 47, 49, 50
Exodus, 63, 68, 71–73

F

Faith, 1, 5, 6, 8, 21, 36, 37, 40, 64, 65, 68, 70, 97, 122, 123, 125, 166–8
Family, 3, 51, 106–8, 112, 145, 164, 174
Family Communion Sunday, 62, 86
Fasting, 113, 168
Fears, 142, 148
Forgiveness, 40–46, 50, 87–89, 91, 92, 119, 126, 157
Francis of Assisi, St., 16
Friendship, 30, 97, 98, 113

G

Gabriel the Archangel, St., 18, 104
Gethsemane, Garden of, 136, 141
Gifts, 9–11, 13, 20, 39, 44, 57–60, 97–99, 101, 132, 159, 166, 169
God
    characteristics of, 67–74, 78–83, 86–94, 147
    chief truths of our faith in, 64, 70
    holy name of, 79, 86, 94, 99
    revelation of, 63, 64, 66–69
    as three persons in one, 66
Goliath, 11
Gospels, 56, 114, 119, 174
Grace, 30–33, 81, 97–99, 101, 115, 119, 144, 159

H

Happiness, 14, 17, 75, 87, 99, 114, 129
Heaven, 33, 35, 72, 73, 74, 76, 97, 99, 112, 115, 146–48, 151, 156, 162–65, 169
Holiness, 14, 15, 17, 78, 79, 163
Holy Family, 103, 105, 106
Holy souls, 162, 164
Holy Spirit, 36–39, 47, 64, 102, 112, 113, 156, 157
    as Church's guide to holiness, 15, 17, 156, 157, 168–69
    as our guide in answering God's call, 1, 36–39, 44, 48, 158–61, 168–69
    as promised and fulfilled by Jesus, 69, 81, 133, 143, 149, 156, 159
Hope, 97, 144
Human beings, 96, 97

I

Incarnation, 102, 108
Isaac, 4
Israel, 84–85, 91
Israelites, 67–69, 71, 73, 75, 80, 87

J

James, St., 22, 136
Jerusalem, 109, 134, 138, 149, 157
Jesus, 7, 81, 160
    baptism of, 111, 112, 118
    birth and early life of, 103–7
    calling of apostles by, 22, 23, 25
    challenge of, to follow as disciples, 1, 36, 44, 69, 106, 149, 157
    in the Eucharist, 51–56, 58, 60, 74, 81, 94, 135
    as healer, 119, 123, 125, 129
    in his forgiving love, 40–42, 47, 48, 69, 99
    in his passion and death, 30, 40, 56, 58, 69, 133, 134, 136–41, 160
    in his public ministry, 42, 43, 111–13
    in his resurrection, 30, 69, 78, 125, 133, 134, 142–45, 148, 160, 165, 169

181

as Judge, 153, 155, 168
kingship of, 150–53, 162, 169
as Light of the World, 105, 106, 108–10, 131, 146
as Messiah, 95, 111, 113, 114, 125, 129
miracles of, 78, 88, 95, 114, 118, 125, 129
    cure of the blind man, 123, 125, 130
    cure of the deaf man, 124
    cure of the leper, 119, 125, 130
    raising of the widow's son, 121, 125
as our help in becoming holy, 14, 15, 17, 99, 108, 160, 161
parables of, 95, 115, 118, 129
    Good Shepherd, 88
    Lost Sheep, 43
    Man Who Built His House on Rock, 54–55
    Mustard Seed, 115, 130
    Pearl of Great Price, 115, 130
    Pharisee and the Tax Collector, 42
    Prodigal Son, 45–46
    Rich Man and Lazarus, 88
Presentation in the Temple of, 105
as Sacrifice at Mass, 52, 53, 56, 58, 141, 168
as Savior and Redeemer, 30, 69, 95, 99, 102–4, 106, 111, 129, 134, 141, 144, 145, 168–70
and the sinful woman, 42–44
teachings of, 35, 43, 69, 126, 132, 143
and Zacchaeus, 43
John the Baptist, 95, 111, 112, 118, 130
John, St., 22, 109, 136, 146, 172, 173
Joseph, St., 102–6
Joy, 36–38, 43, 59, 132, 147
Judas, 137, 140

K

Kindness, 36–38, 44, 90, 155
Kingdom of God, 111, 113–18, 123, 129–33, 150, 153, 157, 162, 169, 172
Kiwanuka, Benedict, 85

L

Last Supper, 51, 56, 135, 140
Laws of love, 75, 77, 88
Lazarus, 147
Leprosy, 119
Life, 96, 97
Liturgy of the Word, 55–56, 58
Love, 30, 35–38, 44, 47, 57, 61, 74–78, 89, 90, 97, 114, 126, 142, 159, 160

M

Manna, 73
Mary, Mother of Jesus, 18–21, 69, 102–6, 108, 133, 156, 169
    as answering God's call, 1, 28, 102, 124
    closeness of, to God, 105, 161, 165, 166
    as intercessor, 18, 165, 166, 169
    as Queen of Heaven and Earth, 165, 166
    role of, in the Church, 18, 21, 28, 60
Mass, 29, 51–53, 57–62, 135, 141, 150, 168, 169, 171
Mercy, 87–90, 154, 155, 166
Miracles, 116. *See also* Jesus, miracles of
Mission of Christians, 111, 118, 128, 149
Missionaries, 110, 149
Moses, 67, 68, 71–73, 75, 78–80, 84, 86, 87, 102
Mother Teresa of Calcutta, 155
Mysteries, 20, 64, 108, 122, 141

N

New Covenant, 135, 141, 168
Nicodemus, 31, 34

O

Obedience, 44, 65, 70, 72, 75, 77, 107, 108, 113, 130
Oil, used in anointing, 11

P

Parents, 44, 107, 108
Parables. *See* Jesus, parables of
Paschal candle, 146
Paschal Mystery, 133
Passion (Palm) Sunday, 134
Passover, 68, 135
Patron saints, 163, 173
Paul, St., 25, 28, 33, 36, 38, 60, 109
Peace, 35–38, 42–44, 49, 50, 61, 62, 87, 88, 132, 144, 150, 166
Penance, 29, 46, 48, 50
Pentecost, 156, 157, 161
Peter, St., 22, 28, 40, 44, 136
Pharaoh, 67, 68, 71, 86
Pilate, Pontius, 137–41
Praise, 10, 12, 13, 78, 86, 93, 174
Prayer, 15, 39, 44, 65, 110, 113, 128, 164
Prayers
    Act of Contrition, 41
    Apostles' Creed, 64
    Come, Holy Spirit, 39
    Eucharistic, 51, 58
    for the Faithful Departed, 169
    Glory to God, 103
    Hail, Holy Queen, 165
    Hail Mary, 20, 21
    Litany of Our Lady, 166
    Our Father, 20, 92, 150
    Psalm Prayers, 73, 83, 87, 93, 94, 99
Priests, 23, 27, 51, 61
Psalms, 12, 13, 73, 83, 87, 92–94, 99, 174
Purgatory, 162, 164, 168, 169

R

Reconciliation. *See* Sacraments, Reconciliation
Religious life, 23, 27, 116
Resurrection. *See* Jesus, in his resurrection
Rosary, 20, 21, 166
Ruth, 7, 8

S

Sacraments, 15, 29, 34, 38
    Baptism, 3, 5, 6, 8, 28, 31, 32, 34, 63, 74, 76, 109–12, 118, 159, 162
    Confirmation, 161
    Eucharist, 29, 34, 39, 51–62, 74, 81, 94, 135, 141, 145, 148, 168
    Reconciliation, 29, 34, 39, 44–50, 119, 125, 171, 174
Sacrifices, 84–85, 110, 113, 115, 118, 128, 132, 135, 141, 157
Saints, 15, 17, 60, 162–67, 169, 173
Samuel, 11
Sarah, 4
Satan, 113, 118, 130. *See also* Devil
Scriptures, 56, 63, 96, 101, 173
Selfishness, 38, 87, 118, 162
Service, 128
Sign of the Cross, 16, 17, 48, 53
Simeon, 95, 105, 108
Sin, 38, 72, 108
    compared to leprosy, 119, 130
    effects of, 88, 120, 162
    nature of, 39, 41, 120
    original, 30, 98, 101, 102
    redemption from, 99, 101, 114, 143, 144
    sorrow for, 40–46, 111
Suffering, 87, 88, 92, 101, 105, 136–39
Sunday, 44, 51, 145, 148, 174

T

Talents, 10–13, 44, 117, 128
Temple, 88, 109
Temptation, 38, 40, 69, 113, 118
Thomas More, St., 85
Trust, 73, 142, 146
Truthfulness, 44

U

Unity with God, 52, 53, 60, 62, 74

W

Water, 31, 32, 34, 138
Wine, 51, 58, 135
Witness, 149, 151
Works of love, 157
Works of mercy, 153
Worship, 93–94

Z

Zacchaeus, 43

SUPPLEMENT

CONTENTS

Reconciliation Booklet

An Advent Project for the Family

Sharing Lent as a Family

The Jesse Tree

Rosary Booklets
    The Glorious Mysteries
    The Sorrowful Mysteries
    The Joyful Mysteries

Scripture Prayer Booklet:
    Gifted with Faith in Baptism

Cutouts

Act of Contrition

My God, I am sorry for my sins with all
    my heart.
In choosing to do wrong
    and failing to do good,
    I have sinned against you
    whom I should love above all things.
I firmly intend, with your help,
    to do penance,
    to sin no more,
    and to avoid whatever leads me to sin.
Our Savior Jesus Christ
    suffered and died for us.
In his name, my God, have mercy.

God Forgives Me

If we admit our sins, Jesus, who is faithful
and just, will forgive them.
                  adapted from 1 John 1:9

Bless the LORD, O my soul;
    and all my being bless his holy name.
I do not forget his goodness to me. He
    forgives me and makes me strong
    again.
He has redeemed my life.
                adapted from Psalm 103:1–5

As I look at Jesus nailed to the cross, I feel sorry for having sinned. I think about how I have failed to show love to God and others.

I Thank God

    I thank you, LORD, with all my heart.
                           Psalm 138:1

Thank you, dear God, for your love and goodness. Thank you for your peace and fatherly forgiveness. I will bring peace to others and try to love them more. I will try to be more like Jesus each day.

Mother Mary, pray for me.
Holy Spirit, help me. Amen.

I do the penance the priest gives me.

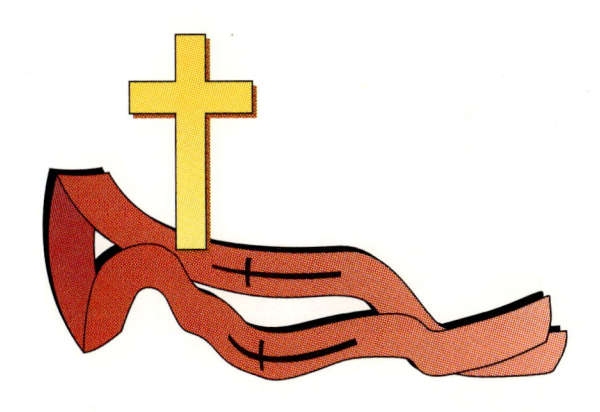

Reconciliation Booklet

"My peace I give to you."

This booklet belongs to

_____

I Examine My Conscience
How Much Do I Love God?
- Do I pray to God? How often?
- Do I use God's name with love? Have I used his name in the wrong way?
- Do I celebrate Mass on Saturday evening or Sunday? Have I missed Sunday Mass deliberately?
- Do I listen well to God's Word?
- Do I thank God for his goodness?
- Do I tell God I am sorry when I have failed to love?
- Do I ask God to help me?
- Have I really been the person Jesus expects me to be?

How Much Do I Love Others?
- Do I obey those who care for me?
- Am I kind and loving? Have I hurt anyone? Do I make up with those I hurt? Do I call others names or make fun of them? Have I been selfish? Do I show respect for myself and others?
- Have I been pure in my thoughts, words, and actions? Do I choose good friends? Am I faithful to them? Have I looked at only good shows and books?
- Am I careful not to waste God's gifts? Am I satisfied with what I have? Do I share? Am I honest? Have I stolen anything? Have I returned it? Have I damaged property? Have I paid for or repaired what I damaged?
- Have I lied to anyone? Have I talked about others in an unkind way? Have I kept promises and secrets?

Prayer to the Holy Spirit
Come, Holy Spirit,
    fill the hearts of your faithful,
    and kindle in them the fire of your love.
Holy Spirit, help me to know how I have loved.
Help me to know how I have failed to love.
Help me to be sorry for failing to love.
Help me to trust in God's loving forgiveness.
                  Amen.

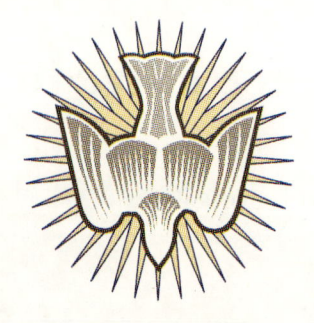

I Make My Confession
The priest welcomes me. I greet him and I make the Sign of the Cross.

The priest says a prayer to help me remember God's forgiving love.

I respond with, "Amen."

The priest may read God's Word.

I make my confession. I may begin, "Forgive me, Father, I have sinned. My last confession was _____ ago."

After telling my sins, I may say, "I am sorry for all my sins."

The priest may tell me how to be more loving. He gives me a penance. I tell God I am sorry in an Act of Contrition.

The priest may say, "Give thanks to the Lord for he is good."

I say, "His mercy endures forever."

An Advent Project for the Family

Advent means "coming." During Advent all Christians prepare to celebrate the coming of Jesus, our Savior. Make Advent a time of prayerful waiting for the celebration of Christ's birth by making a family Jesse Tree.

All the decorations on the Jesse Tree remind us of people who waited for the coming of Jesus. The tree is named after a man from Bethlehem. One of Jesse's sons became the most important king of Israel, King David. God had promised that the Savior would belong to the family of King David. As we decorate the Jesse Tree, we remember God's promise to send us a Savior.

Tear out carefully the Jesse Tree on page 191. Mount it on stiff paper to hang where it will remind everyone to get ready for Jesus' birthday. Decorate the tree at once or add a decoration each day for nine days.

Adam and Eve

God gave Adam and Eve a share in his own divine life. They were very happy until they sinned by disobeying God. God loved them even after they had sinned, however. He promised to send a Savior.

Many years passed before God sent Jesus as Savior, but God's promise began with Adam and Eve. That is why we put a symbol of Adam and Eve on the Jesse Tree.

Read Psalm 100 and draw an apple in Adam and Eve's circle on the Jesse Tree.

Noah

Adam and Eve's children sinned too. So many people sinned that it seemed everyone forgot about loving God.

1

Joseph

Joseph, the man chosen by God to be the foster father of Jesus, belonged to the family of King David. He lived many hundreds of years after King David died. Joseph, a carpenter, was a good and holy man. God knew that he would take loving care of Jesus and Mary.

Read Matthew 1:18–22 and draw a hammer in Joseph's circle on the Jesse Tree.

Mary

When the time was right to send the Savior to his people, God chose a mother to love and care for his Son and help him grow. God chose Mary, a young Jewish woman, to be the mother of Jesus.

God our Father kept the promise he had made to Adam and Eve. On Christmas day, in the little town of Bethlehem, the Savior was born.

Read Luke 1:26–34 and draw a flower in Mary's circle on the Jesse Tree.

Jesus

Put a large *P* in the top circle of the Jesse Tree. Cross the *P* with an X to form ☧, a symbol for Christ the Savior. Use your tree to tell the story of those who prepared for the coming of the Lord. Then pray:

Lord Jesus,
You fill our hearts with your love.
Help us during Advent to bring
Your love and joy to others. Amen.

4

God told Noah, a good man, that a flood would destroy all the evil in the world. Noah was to build an ark to save himself, his family, and two of every kind of animal. After the Flood God promised never again to destroy the earth that way. As a sign of his promise, God showed Noah a rainbow.

Read Genesis 9:8–17 and draw a rainbow and an ark in Noah's circle on the Jesse Tree.

Abraham

Long after the Flood, God called Abraham to be the father of his chosen people. God told Abraham to leave his home and his country. In return God promised to make Abraham the father of many nations. He told Abraham that the children of his family would be as countless as the stars. Abraham believed God and did as God asked. Abraham became the father of the Jewish people.

Read Genesis 15:1–6 and add stars to Abraham's circle on the Jesse Tree.

Joseph

Before the Savior came, the Jewish family grew in number. One member, Jacob, had twelve sons. Joseph was his favorite. When Jacob gave Joseph a coat of many colors, Joseph's brothers became envious. One day, while out watching the sheep, they sold Joseph as a slave to travelers to Egypt. The brothers told Jacob that a wild animal had killed his son.

In Egypt God cared for Joseph by making him a friend of Pharaoh. Joseph helped the Egyptians when a great famine came over the land. Because Joseph had stored food when the crops were good, he had enough to keep the Egyptians from starving during this difficult time.

Joseph's father and brothers did not have enough food in their land either. Jacob sent his sons to Egypt for food. There Joseph was kind. He forgave his brothers for selling him as a slave. He told them to bring all their families to Egypt where they would all have enough to eat.

Read Acts 7:9–14 and draw a coat of many colors in Joseph's circle on the Jesse Tree.

Moses

Many years after Joseph died, the pharaoh of Egypt began to fear that the families of Joseph's relatives would become powerful in his land. He made all the Jewish people slaves. For a long, long time God's chosen people lived as slaves in Egypt. Their life was very hard, but God did not forget them. He sent Moses to lead them to freedom. Through Moses God set his people free. Then he gave Moses laws to guide his people. We call these laws the Ten Commandments.

Read Deuteronomy 7:6–9 and put the tablets of the Ten Commandments in Moses' circle on the Jesse Tree.

David

Moses led the Jewish people to the land that God had promised Abraham so many years before. Then God gave the people kings to rule them.

The greatest king was David. As a boy David had been a shepherd in the fields near Bethlehem. As a king David was good and wise. God promised David that the Savior would belong to his family.

Read Acts 13:22–23 and draw a crown in David's circle on the Jesse Tree.

Sharing Lent as a Family

During Lent we should recall our own Baptism and renew our Christian life. The Church urges us to spend time each day considering the mystery of God's love, as shown especially in the suffering, death, and resurrection of Jesus. To help you make these weeks of Lent a time of spiritual growth, we suggest the following activities.

Ash Wednesday
Talk about what you as a family can do to make each day of Lent a special time for following Christ. On small pieces of paper have family members write down one thing each that they would like to improve in, or eliminate from, their lives. On the other side of the paper slips, have them write their names. After Lent these slips may be returned so that family members can evaluate how well they kept their promises.

The Pretzel
The pretzel—made from flour, water, and salt—reminds us that, a long time ago, people fasted from milk, butter, eggs, cheese, cream, and meat during Lent. They made the small breads we call pretzels in the shape of arms crossed in prayer. Serve this special Lenten food during Lent as a reminder that this season is a time for special prayer as well as for fasting.

Reading the Bible
Daily Scripture reading can help you form your priorities and attitudes as you come to understand better the Lord's love for you.

Holy Thursday
Make Holy Thursday a day of loving self-giving as you recall Christ's complete offering of himself on Calvary and in the Holy Eucharist.

The Holy Thursday meal can recall the Passover that led to freedom from slavery. Many simplified versions of this ceremonial dinner, known as the *seder meal*, are available for families to use. Plan to attend the parish Holy Thursday evening liturgy as a family.

Good Friday
Make a worship center by setting up a crucifix in an appropriate place. Let the children place some sign of their appreciation for Christ's love near the crucifix. The sign can be toys with which they will not play for the sacred three hours of Good Friday, a letter written to the Lord, or a container that has the mission money gathered from the sacrifices they have made during Lent.

If possible, attend the Good Friday liturgy to express love for Jesus, who showed his love for us on the day he died.

Easter Vigil
Easter is not simply one feast among many. It is *the* feast of the year and can be truly celebrated as such by those who have prepared their hearts during Lent. Decorate your table with a baptismal robe and candle. Renew your baptismal promises as a family. Talk about the Paschal candle that will be seen in church at Mass during the Easter season. Try to be present at the parish celebration of the Easter Vigil.

As you pick up your family Bible, make a triple Sign of the Cross on your forehead, lips, and heart, praying as you do so, "The Lord be in my thoughts, on my lips, and in my heart." Invite the children to repeat this prayer after you. Read the Gospel for the next day's Mass and discuss what the Lord is asking you to do to bring his message to the people you meet each day.

Close your discussion with the words of the Israelites when Moses gave them the Word of the Lord: "All that the Lord has said, we will heed and do" (Exodus 24:7). Then reverently place the Bible in its special place, saying, "Happy are those who hear the Word of God and keep it."

Sacrifice

Sacrifice, a word commonly associated with Lent, comes from two Latin words that mean "to make holy." Prayerful reflection and family discussion of Isaiah 58:1–9 can help your family decide how to respond more fully to the Lord with Lenten sacrifices. Money saved can be given to relieve social injustices. Many families eat a "poverty meal" once a week during Lent and donate the savings from this, together with those from their other Lenten sacrifices, to groups devoted to the missions or to the liberation of the poor and powerless.

The Rosary

Pray at least one of the sorrowful mysteries each day. As a family, reflect on how our thoughtless treatment of others continues the suffering of Christ even today. Then pray the decade, asking our Blessed Mother's help in overcoming those faults and sins that hurt others.

Way of the Cross

Follow Christ's way of love by going from station to station in church, or meditate on each station in your own home. Specific prayers are not required when we make the Way of the Cross. Simply reflect upon Jesus' journey of love. (Pictures in booklets can help children become familiar with the stations.)

When contemplating the stations, discuss what happened at each station, what the event tells us about Jesus' love, and how the difficulties you experience each day relate to Jesus' sufferings. End each meditation with a prayer for help to follow Christ's way of love.

Making Holy Week Special
Passion Sunday (Palm Sunday)

The palms we receive in church on the last Sunday of Lent remind us that when Christ our King entered Jerusalem, the people acclaimed him and waved palms in welcome. Have a procession during which you place blessed palms in each room of your home. Say as you do so, "Praise and honor to you, Lord Jesus Christ, King of endless glory." Have your family repeat the acclamation. End your procession with a discussion of what your family will do to celebrate Holy Week.

The Jesse Tree

- Jesus
- Mary
- Joseph
- David
- Joseph
- Moses
- Adam and Eve
- Noah
- Abraham

Fourth Glorious Mystery: The Assumption

After Jesus' death Mary helps the apostles. When her life on earth ends, Jesus takes her, body and soul, into heaven. He does this because he loves his mother very much and because she has never sinned.

Let us ask Mary to help us so that we may one day share in her glory.

First Glorious Mystery: The Resurrection

Jesus rises from the dead on the third day. He is seen by his mother, Mary Magdalene, and the apostles. To the apostle Thomas he says, "Blessed are those who have not seen and have believed."

Let us tell Jesus that we believe in him.

Color a bead each time you say your prayers.

The Glorious Mysteries

My Rosary Book

Second Glorious Mystery: The Ascension

Before Jesus ascends into heaven, he tells his apostles to teach the Good News and baptize people everywhere. He tells them to wait for the Holy Spirit. Then he ascends into heaven to prepare a place for everyone.

Let us tell Jesus that we hope to live with him in heaven some day.

Third Glorious Mystery: The Coming of the Holy Spirit

Mary and the disciples wait and pray for the Holy Spirit to come. When he comes, tongues of fire can be seen above the head of each of the disciples. The Spirit fills their hearts with great love and courage.

Let us ask the Holy Spirit to make our love stronger.

Prayers for the Rosary

Apostles' Creed
I believe in God, the Father almighty, creator of heaven and earth. I believe in Jesus Christ, his only Son, our Lord. He was conceived by the power of the Holy Spirit and born of the Virgin Mary. He suffered under Pontius Pilate, was crucified, died, and was buried. He descended to the dead. On the third day he rose again. He ascended into heaven and is seated at the right hand of the Father. He will come again to judge the living and the dead. I believe in the Holy Spirit, the holy catholic Church, the communion of saints, the forgiveness of sins, the resurrection of the body, and the life everlasting. Amen.

Our Father
Hail Mary
Doxology

Fifth Glorious Mystery: The Crowning of Mary

Jesus honors Mary in heaven. She is crowned Queen of Heaven and Earth. She watches over us and prays for us.

Let us ask Mary to help us grow in love for Jesus.

Third Joyful Mystery: The Birth of Christ

The Son of God becomes the child Jesus. Mary is holding him in her arms. St. Joseph is standing nearby, watching over them. See how much Mary and Joseph love the child Jesus!

Let us ask Mary to help us grow in love for Jesus.

Prayers for the Rosary

Apostles' Creed
I believe in God, the Father almighty, creator of heaven and earth. I believe in Jesus Christ, his only Son, our Lord. He was conceived by the power of the Holy Spirit and born of the Virgin Mary. He suffered under Pontius Pilate, was crucified, died, and was buried. He descended to the dead. On the third day he rose again. He ascended into heaven and is seated at the right hand of the Father. He will come again to judge the living and the dead. I believe in the Holy Spirit, the holy catholic Church, the communion of saints, the forgiveness of sins, the resurrection of the body, and the life everlasting. Amen.

Our Father
Hail Mary
Doxology

Fifth Joyful Mystery: The Finding of Jesus

Jesus is missing for three days. How happy Mary and Joseph are to find him in the Temple. Jesus goes home with them and obeys them.

Let us ask Mary to teach us how to obey as Jesus did.

The Joyful Mysteries

My Rosary Book

First Joyful Mystery: The Annunciation

Mary is listening as the angel Gabriel speaks to her. He tells Mary that God has chosen her to be the mother of his Son. Mary says, "Yes, I will do as God wills."

Let us ask Mary to help us say yes to all that God asks.

Second Joyful Mystery: The Visitation

See how happy Mary and Elizabeth are! Mary has come to help her relative Elizabeth. Elizabeth is honored to have Mary, the mother of the Savior, visit her.

Let us ask Mary to help us be kind to others, especially older people.

How to Pray the Rosary

1. Hold the crucifix and make the Sign of the Cross with it.
2. Say the Apostles' Creed while holding the cross.
3. On the first bead, say the Our Father.
4. On each of the three beads, say a Hail Mary for more faith, hope, and love.
5. Say the Doxology (Glory Be) on the chain before the large bead.
6. Call to mind the first mystery and think about it. Say the Our Father on the first bead.
7. On each of the ten beads, say a Hail Mary. Keep the picture of the mystery in your mind.
8. After each ten Hail Marys, say the Doxology.
9. Say each decade the same way, thinking about each mystery.
10. After the last Doxology you may bless yourself with the crucifix and kiss it.

Fourth Joyful Mystery: The Presentation

Simeon comes to the Temple to pray every day. He tells God how happy he is to see the child Jesus. He says that Jesus will be a light for everyone.

Let us ask Mary to teach us how to pray.

Gifted with Faith in Baptism

This book belongs to

_____

Community Counts
Think and pray about these . . .

Children, obey your parents in everything, for this is pleasing to the Lord. Col 3:20

Bear one another's burdens, and so you will fulfill the law of Christ. Gal 6:2

Humbly regard others as more important than yourselves. from Phil 2:3

You are in our hearts. from 2 Cor 7:3

I give thanks to my God through Jesus Christ for all of you. from Rom 1:8

Set an example for those who believe, in speech, conduct, love, faith, and purity. from 1 Tm 4:12

Rejoice always. 1 Thes 5:16

God . . . causes the growth. from 1 Cor 3:7

I have called you by name:

_____

(Write your name here.)

You are **mine**.
You are **precious** in my eyes.
I love you.

Isaiah 43:1, 4

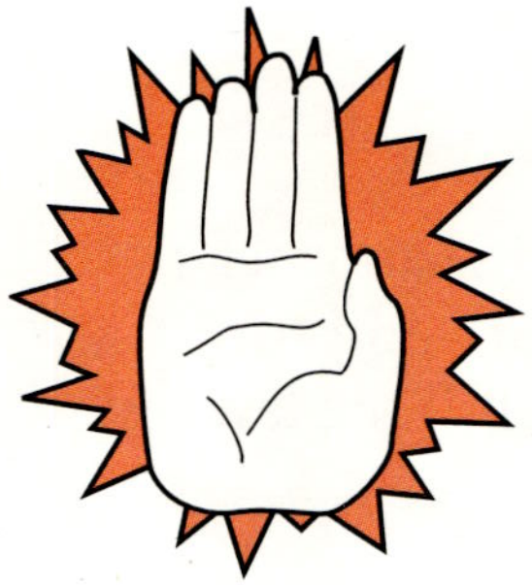

Hold It!

Put these Scripture verses into your own words.

Turn to me and be safe, all you ends of the earth, for I am God; there is no other!
Isaiah 45:22

_____
_____

He who walks uprightly is safe, but he whose ways are crooked falls into the pit.
Proverbs 28:18

_____
_____

A kind mouth multiplies friends.
from Sirach 6:5

_____
_____

Let another praise you—not your own mouth; someone else—not your own lips.
Proverbs 27:2

_____
_____

Live in a manner worthy of the call you have received.
from Ephesians 4:1

_____
_____

Color a block every time you use this booklet.

The name of Jesus is a prayer.

Look at the picture and repeat, "Jesus."

3

Jesus, forgive me.

For times . . .
　When I did not listen to the Holy Spirit . . .
　When I did not pray . . .
　When I did not desire forgiveness of sins . . .
　When I did not obey . . . .
　When I hurt others . . .
　When I damaged or wasted your gifts . . .
　When I was selfish . . . .
　When I did not say, "I am sorry," for hurting someone's feelings . . .

You, Lord, who know the hearts of all (Acts 1:24). . . . Forgive me. . . . Fill me with grace and power.

10

Draw what these Scripture

"I am the light of the world. Whoever follows me will not walk in darkness." John 8:12

"Prepare the way of the LORD." Isaiah 40:3

Pray the psalms—prayers Jesus prayed.

Psalm 62:2–3

My soul rests in God alone,
  from whom comes my salvation.
God alone is my rock and salvation,
  my secure height; I shall never fall.

Psalm 18:2–4

I love you, LORD, my strength,
LORD, my rock, my fortress, my deliverer,
My God, my rock of refuge,
  my shield, . . . my stronghold!
Praised be the LORD, I exclaim!

Psalm 40:2–4

I waited, waited for the LORD;
  who bent down and heard my cry,
Drew me . . . out of the mud of the swamp,
Set my feet upon rock . . .
And put a new song in my mouth,
  a hymn to our God.
Many shall look on in awe
  and they shall trust in the LORD.

verses mean to you.

"Do not worry about your life and what you will eat, or about your body and what you will wear."   Luke 12:22

"I have enjoyed God's help to this very day."   Acts 26:22

5

Write under each host the name of a person for whom you want to pray. When you do pray for that person, color the cross on the host.

Love one another as I love you.
John 15:12

8

Prayers Borrowed from Scripture

Write when you might use these prayers.

"My Lord and my God!"

John 20:28

_____

"Lord, save me!"

Matthew 14:30

_____

"Master, we have worked hard all night and have caught nothing, but at your command, I will lower the nets."

Luke 5:5

_____

"If you wish, you can make me clean."

Mark 1:40

_____

"Lord, please let me see."

Luke 18:41

_____

"My soul proclaims the greatness of the Lord."

Luke 1:46

_____

"Lord, do not trouble yourself, for I am not worthy to have you enter under my roof . . . but say the word and let my servant be healed."

Luke 7:6, 7

_____

Made by God with Love

Chapter 1

Chapter 6

Chapter 3

Chapter 2

My Talent:

Name

Chapter 7

© Loyola Press

© Loyola Press

© Loyola Press

© Loyola Press

© Loyola Press

Chapter 9

Chapter 13

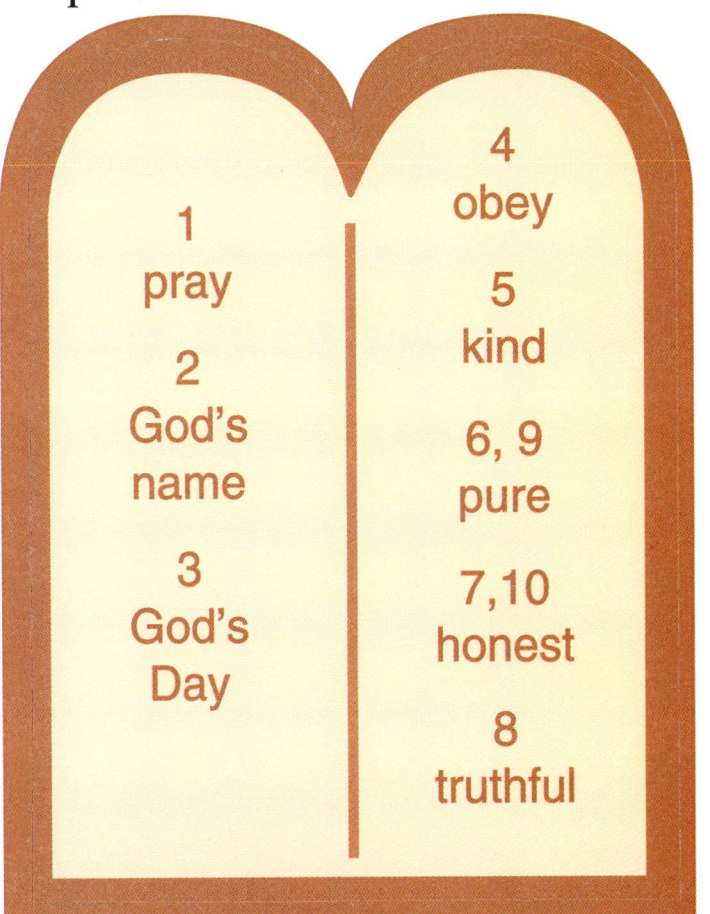

1 pray	4 obey
2 God's name	5 kind
3 God's Day	6, 9 pure
	7, 10 honest
	8 truthful

Chapter 17

Be an Apostle of Prayer

Offer your love to Jesus each day by praying the Morning Offering. Offer all you do during the day to Jesus.

Directions

Tear out the heart.
Staple or glue the heart to one end of a drinking straw. Poke a hole in the bottom of a paper cup and push the other end of the straw into it.

All for you, Most Sacred Heart of Jesus

© Loyola Press

© Loyola Press

Morning Offering

O Jesus,
through the Immaculate Heart of Mary,
I offer you my prayers, works, joys,
and sufferings of this day
in union with the Holy Sacrifice
of the Mass throughout the world.
I offer them for all the intentions
of Your Sacred Heart.
Amen.

© Loyola Press